FINDING · VERMONT

FINDING · VERMONT

An Informal Guide to Vermont's Places and People

By Tom Slayton

Vermont Life Magazine
Montpelier, Vermont

First Edition.   1 2 3 4 5 6 7 8 9 10

Book design by Jan Hubbard/Battery Graphics
Maps by Armand Poulin.
Frontispiece, Tunbridge by Kindra Clineff

"The Village" from *A Mountain Township* by Walter Hard. Copyright 1933, 1950, 1963 by Walter Hard. Reprinted by permission of Vermont Books, Middlebury, VT, publisher.

"Spring Pools" from *The Poetry of Robert Frost*, edited by Edward Connery Lathem. Copyright 1928, © 1969 by Holt, Rinehart and Winston. Copyright © 1956 by Robert Frost. Reprinted by permission of Henry Holt and Company.

Quoted matter on pages 63-65 from *Outsiders Inside Vermont* by T.D. Seymour Bassett, published by Phoenix Publishing, Canaan, NH. Copyright © 1967 by T.D. Seymour Bassett. Reprinted by permission of the author.

Library of Congress Cataloging-in-Publication Data
Slayton, Tom, 1941-
        Finding Vermont.
        Bibliography: p.
        1. Vermont—Description and travel—1981 —Guidebooks. I. Title.
F47.3.S54 1986   917.43′0443   86-23372
ISBN 0-936896-07-8

CONTENTS

Paul Miller

Spring, and the voice of the tractor is heard in the land. Small farms
contribute much to Vermont's character.

SHAPED BY SMALLNESS

V ermont's long-standing love of hog-on-ice independence and individual freedom is founded in its history and traditions. Like Texas, where contrariness and a certain self-consciousness are also virtues, Vermont was an independent republic before it became a state. But Texas, for obvious reasons, expresses its independence in a love of bigness. Vermont, for reasons that may be equally obvious, has chosen to celebrate through smallness.

In that respect, it has developed a different set of values from the prevailing American ethic. Writer Sinclair Lewis noted that fact in 1929 when he told a Rutland audience:

> I like Vermont because it is quiet, because you have a population that is solid and not driven mad by the American mania—that mania which considers a town of 4,000 twice as good as a town of 2,000. Following that reasoning, one would get the charming paradox that Chicago would be 10 times better than the entire state of Vermont, but I have been in Chicago, and have not found it so.

Obviously, Vermont is small, comprising about 9,600 square miles and slightly more than a half-million people. It is also statistically the most rural state in the country because 66 percent of its people—a higher percentage than in any other state—live in "rural" settings. Rural, according to the federal government, means any village with less than 2,500 residents. Vermont's largest city, Burlington, has about 40,000 people, fewer than Albany, N.Y., or Manchester, N.H.

Less obviously, Vermont humor tends to be the humor of understatement, which is the humor people use when they know each other and the "rules" of local living well. Vermonters have lived close to one another for a long time. Even on farms, neighbors have often been neighbors for a long time. It is probably no coincidence that humor in the west, where everyone was quite recently a stranger, is the humor of overstatement, the tall tale.

In talk and writing, superlatives are shunned. The "usually" and "probably" in that last paragraph are a Vermonter's conditioning, a habitual hedge against the uncertainties of weather and circumstance. Former *Vermont Life* editor Walter Hard Jr.

once wrote that if a Vermonter "guesses" something—as in "I guess it's goin' t' rain . . . " — that's about as certain as he or she will ever be.

Naturally, any state with a total population smaller than most middle-sized American cities, a tradition of family-run farms and a community experience based on small village life, has to come to grips with a reduced scale somehow. The surprising thing is that the experience has been so pleasant. Vermont has followed, in the words of its adopted poet laureate Robert Frost, the "road less traveled by," and has liked the route well enough to want to continue.

For one thing, that alternate route has meant and still means that life is lived on a controllable scale; smaller stores, smaller schools, towns where people actually know one another and can find a place to park their cars add up to less pressure and less confusion. While smallness can mean a sense of smothering confinement, it can also mean intimacy. Vermont sometimes seems like a single village in which everyone knows and at times even likes almost everyone else. The state's governors are accessible and answer to "Phil," or "Deane," or "Dick," or more recently "Madeleine." They still answer their own telephones at home, and those phones are listed in Vermont's thin regional phonebooks along with everyone else's.

There is no executive mansion in Vermont, which is what one would expect from a state where the dominant political institutions are a low-paid citizens' legislature that meets for roughly 16 weeks each winter and the intensely local annual free-for-all known as town meeting.

There is a negative side to smallness. Small villages can be ingrown and gossipy. One-room schools may harbor grossly inadequate education. Ten-cow hill farms have at times produced blighted hopes and thwarted lives. But often it seems that small towns, small schools, small valleys with small farms and small churches, all overseen by a small state government—a world, that is, of limits willingly accepted—manages to create the very thing the modern, large, predominately urban world lacks and needs most: that sense of human contact and understanding called community.

"Smallness has meant to the state a sense of intimacy," notes Washington County Sen. William Doyle, a political science teacher from Johnson State College when he isn't serving in the state Senate. "When people know each other, they tend to trust each other, and because statewide politicians are available and are known, they tend to be trusted by the people who elect them."

Vermont may have an advantage even in national political arenas, Doyle believes, because by re-electing capable people repeatedly to the U.S. Senate, those senators can become powerful in an arena where even a small state like Vermont has equal representation. Sen. George D. Aiken, the nineteenth century Sen. Justin Morrill, and others are examples.

Smallness also insures responsive politicians because of the fervent interest many Vermonters have in local and state politics, and the close scrutiny they therefore give their representative's every vote. And that principle applies to other aspects of life as well.

To know the teacher who teaches your children, the lawyer who writes your deed, the legislator who writes your laws, the grocer who sells you your food and in some instances the farmer who grows it does not make either them or you any better a person. But it can make both of you more responsible, more *decent*, if you will.

That does not mean that life in Vermont is any more pleasant or more painful than anyplace else. At times, though, it seems clearer, more comprehensible, even universally so. As the poet Walter Hard once wrote, in his poem, "The Village":

> There the whole of life unfolds
> From childhood's carefree days
> To that hillside with the white stones.
> Fifty houses, offering the life of the race.

THE MOUNTAINS THAT MADE VERMONT

V ermont's geographical isolation from the American mainstream has shaped it in profound ways. First a forbidding wilderness and later a quiet and hard-to-get-to corner of New England, Vermont spent a long time largely on its own. That has now changed, and the Green Mountains are more closely linked than ever to the rest of the United States. But the distinctive attitudes bred by Vermont's history and isolation remain: a love of independence, a respect for nature, a long-standing affection for small-town community life, a variety of rural traditions.

In the summer from the air, Vermont looks like a huge, rumpled green rug with the rumples all running north and south. That is actually not a bad way to think of the state topographically. Bounded on the east and west by valleys, Vermont takes its nickname from the immense rumple that runs its length, the Green Mountains. They are its dominant physical feature and have shaped both history and society.

For many years, the mountains were a powerful barrier to trade, transportation and communication; they effectively split Vermont into east-side/west-side components. The governorship alternated regularly between east and west during the nineteenth century. Even the traditional Vermont accents are different east and west of the mountains. One reason Montpelier, near dead-center, became the capital was because it was an unprepossessing little town regarded as a compromise between east-siders and west-siders.

The mountains began about 500 million years ago as ocean bottom. Sediments laid down over the eons by the ancient seas turned into rock, and those layers of rock were, in turn, heaved up by intercontinental geophysical forces into huge mountain complexes that may have been as high or higher than today's geologically "young" mountains—the Himalayas. The Green Mountains, along with the rest of the eastern Appalachian chain of which they are a part, later eroded, over millions of years. The Green Mountains we see today are but the stumps of earlier giants.

Wind, rain, weather and rivers wore down the mountains, and the final touches that we can still see today came from a relatively recent phenomenon—the last great

Mottled with shadows, Camel's Hump broods over a fertile valley near Ferrisburg.

Ice Age, which ended about 10,000 years ago. Because of climatic changes, a great wave of ice crept down upon Vermont from Labrador. At its highest point, it rose a mile high, possibly two miles, towering far above the peaks of all of Vermont's mountains. The ice covered all of New England and most of what is now the northern United States. Its immense weight scoured the landscape, stripping boulders and bedrock from mountain and valley alike.

The evidence of past glaciation is everywhere in Vermont. Heavy striations atop Mount Mansfield and other rocky peaks, the ice-plucked, south-facing cliff of Camel's Hump, and the rounded hillocks and smooth sides of the Champlain and Connecticut Valleys all offer evidence of our ice-sculpted geologic past. Chipman Hill in Middlebury is a conical glacial hill or *kame*; the large gravelly plateau that is the site of both the Burlington Airport and the University of Vermont's Centennial Field is a glacial plain; a winding glacial ridge or *esker* begins in Windsor and wanders some 24 miles into New Hampshire. The gravel pits used by town highway departments for roadwork are often extracted from glacial deposits; geologists have on occasion had to hustle to protect significant glacial formations from being dug up and spread upon Vermont's back roads by well-meaning road crews.

Geologists identify six major physiographic regions in the state. Two of them are mountain ranges, the Taconics in southwestern Vermont and the Green Mountains, running the length of the state and encompassing several smaller ranges. Two of the other four regions are valleys. The Vermont Valley is a narrow, scenic defile between the Green Mountains and the parallel Taconics in southwestern Vermont; the Champlain Valley to the north is a broad swatch of rich farm land that dominates Vermont's northwest. Most of the land east of the Green Mountains is in the hilly Vermont Piedmont region. The Northeastern Highlands region, which corresponds approximately with Essex County in the far northeastern corner of the state, is closely akin, geologically, to northern New Hampshire.

Each region has its own story; the Taconics, for example, are thought to be the tops of the ancient Green Mountains, upthrust geologically and pushed westward as a giant slab of stone, some 8,000 feet thick, eons ago. The geologic roots of the Taconics are thought to be about 40 miles to the east of where the mountains themselves now stand, the eroded fragments of an immense geologic upheaval. The Vermont Valley, historically a major thoroughfare into the state, was formed by primordial rivers eroding the land between the two major mountain ranges. Geographer Harold Meeks notes that the northeastern part of the state is still, in effect, frontier Vermont. Most of it is heavily forested and sparsely settled.

But the geographical factor that has probably had the greatest influence on Vermont's history (at least its history since the coming of European settlers) has probably been its isolation. From the first, Vermont has been off the beaten track.

Why did Vermont remain relatively isolated from the rest of America for so long? The Green Mountains are one obvious answer; they not only made travel difficult for people trying to get into Vermont, they in effect subdivided the state itself. But there were other factors also.

Unlike any other state in New England, Vermont has no seacoast, and that meant as much to its lack of development as did the spine of mountains down its center. The nearly impenetrable forest that covered most of the state played a part in the early years. Vermont was regarded as a wild frontier long after southern New England was settled and civilized. Even after the land was cleared and roads were built through the mountains, opportunity was limited by climate and the stone-ridden mountain soils. Although many farms were prosperous, many were not, and none could compare with the broad, flat lands of the midwest. The push of American empire went westward.

Much of the hustle and urban development of the late 1800s and early 1900s passed Vermont by; its scale remained small, its traditions rural. It was not until after World War II that the twentieth century really arrived in Vermont, via modern highways and mass communication networks. Both Vermont's delay in joining mainstream America and its recent acceptance of that process have had a tremendous impact on the way Vermont looks and the ways Vermonters think.

WILDERNESS IN VERMONT

V ermont's mountains are no longer a barrier between eastern and western Vermont. In the past 50 years, they have become a place of recreation for skiers, hikers, hunters and fishermen from Vermont and elsewhere. They are an economic resource.

Vermont had its share of mountaintop hotels in the 1800s, but the era of modern mountain recreation can probably be traced to 1909, when the associate principal of Vermont Academy, James Taylor, watched the mist clear from Stratton Mountain and dreamed of a trail running the length of the Green Mountain range, linking all the major summits. The Green Mountain Club had its first meeting in Burlington the next year, and by 1931 the trail Taylor envisioned—The Long Trail—was completed, a "Footpath in the Wilderness" running 265 miles between Massachusetts and Canada. Vermont's mountains have rightly been regarded as prime hiking territory ever since.

Though neither as high nor as imposing as the White Mountains of New Hampshire or the Adirondacks in upstate New York, the Green Mountains offer many delightful walks and views. They are friendly mountains, accessible enough for a day hike, yet challenging enough for an extended backpacking or skiing adventure. Several of the higher peaks offer striking vistas from their rocky promontories.

Hiking developed in the Green Mountains because Vermonters saw that mountains in upstate New York and New Hampshire brought tourists, economic activity, and ultimately, dollars to those states. Although Vermont's mountains were smaller, Vermonters felt their beauty should be promoted, too. The state has succeeded beyond its promoters' wildest dreams, but for reasons Vermonters could not have foreseen—the recreation explosion after World War II, and specifically, the growth of skiing.

With their moderate slopes and heavy natural snow cover, Vermont's mountains are well suited to commercial skiing. Vermont state government helped the development of commercial skiing by opening some public lands for ski development and building access roads. Skiing flourished, eclipsing mountain hiking in economic importance. More recently, concerned by the scale of some ski-related developments,

Louis Borie

Hikers on Mount Mansfield's rocky spine can look out over mile upon mile of ridges, valleys, lakes and forests.

the state responded with environmental laws that attempt to keep mountain development within reasonable bounds.

In the 1970s and 1980s cross-country skiing has added a new recreational element. The Catamount Ski Trail running the length of Vermont is now under development, offering a contemporary parallel to the Long Trail.

Some of the most interesting mountains in Vermont with hiking trails are the following:

- **Mount Mansfield.** A two-mile-long treeless summit ridge covered with rare alpine plants culminates in the state's highest peak, 4,393 feet high, with views in all directions. Most ski development here has been kept off the summit ridge, so much of the mountain's wild character remains unspoiled. The mountain is a fascinating area for an afternoon's hike or a week's backpacking, but walk carefully, much of the area is fragile, especially above timberline.
- **The Willoughby Lake Mountains.** Neither Mount Pisgah (elev. 2,751 ft.) nor Mount Hor (elev. 2,648 ft.) is particularly high, even by Vermont standards. Yet they offer fine views of one of the most spectacular lakes in the Northeast and both have interesting hiking trails. Hor is the easier of the two; neither should be attempted in spring.
- **Camel's Hump.** The state's most striking mountain remains undeveloped, though accessible by hiking trails from all sides. It culminates in a 4,083-foot rocky summit covered with rare alpine flora (fragile) and has a spectacular cliff on its south face. In recent years the mountain has become a living laboratory for acid rain research.
- **Mount Hunger.** This rocky peak in the Worcester Range (elev. 3,620 ft.) offers spectacular views of the main Green Mountain range to the west, nearby villages and farm land and, on clear days, of the White Mountains to the east. Its rocky summit was bared when a forest fire swept over the mountaintop about 50 years ago.
- **Lincoln Mountain.** This four-mile-long series of peaks is a challenging but rewarding hike along a high mountaintop ridge. The Long Trail pokes in and out of

forest cover here and the views are delightful. Athletes may want to hike the 11 miles from Lincoln Gap to Appalachian Gap (Route 17) in a single day. For the less fanatical but fit, a trip up Mount Abraham (elev. 4,052 ft.) from Lincoln Gap and back is a little over five miles, with a spectacular view from the rocky summit. Old-time Vermonters still call this mountain "Potato Hill" because of its shape.

- **Mount Ascutney** (elev. 3,144 ft.). An isolated peak overlooking the Connecticut Valley, Ascutney has special hiking traditions of its own to complement its striking beauty. It also has a road going to its summit.
- **Blue Ridge Mountain** (elev. 3,278 ft.). This little-known mountain just east of Rutland offers a moderate hike through pretty forest and unusual views of Pico Peak and the surrounding territory.
- **Mount Equinox** (elev. 3,816 ft.). Another mountain with a road, Equinox is the highest peak in the Taconics. Although its summit is fairly heavily developed, it is the highest peak overlooking the Vermont Valley, and offers striking views in all directions. From the summit, a secluded Carthusian monastery can be seen on the west side of the mountain, and several wind generators line the high ridge.
- **Stratton Mountain** (elev. 3,936 ft.). Although a major ski area is located here, much of Stratton Mountain remains pleasingly wild, and there are links to a surprising amount of Vermont history (including a speech by Daniel Webster in 1840 when this was very prosperous logging country).
- **Harmon Hill** (elev. 2,325 ft.). Just east of Bennington, its grassy summit offers a pleasant view and is an ideal picnicking spot. The climb is a bit steep in the beginning.

ABENAKIS: The First Vermonters

For years the prevailing belief was that Vermont had never been a permanent home to Native American peoples, but had been a "land between," a buffer territory between the Iroquois and Algonkian nations. Even as careful a writer as Dorothy Canfield Fisher perpetuated that myth in her book, *Vermont Tradition*, and virtually every historian repeated it until the 1970s brought systematic modern archaeological methods to Vermont. In 1965, Canadian scholar Gordon C. Day published "The Indian Occupation of Vermont," an article based on modern research that destroyed the "no-man's-land" myth once and for all, and in 1981, the publication of *The Original Vermonters* by two University of Vermont professors, William A. Haviland and Marjorie W. Power, systematically explored and interpreted the culture of Vermont's first inhabitants, the Paleoindians and their likely descendants, the Western Abenakis.

Today, historians have documentation that Vermont's first people, the Paleo-indians, lived here shortly after the retreat of the glaciers of the last ice age, and that Native American cultures flourished and developed for thousands of years—roughly until the coming of the white man. The first people arrived in Vermont sometime after 10,000 B.C., when the massive glacier that had covered all of New England retreated. Their occupancy can be broken into Paleoindian, Archaic, and Woodland periods; archaeologists believe that the inhabitants of the later periods were descendants of the earlier people who slowly changed their way of life to meet changing environmental conditions.

By the first millenium A.D., several major bands of people historically called the Western Abenakis lived in Vermont. They built good-sized villages of a few hundred people on canoeable streams near the major bodies of water, where, according to Haviland and Power, they lived a life of seasonal subsistence, farming, fishing, and gathering through the spring and summer, and hunting through the fall and winter. Abenaki villages were located in western Vermont near the mouths of Otter Creek, the Winooski, the Lamoille and the Missisquoi rivers. There were also two major bands in the Connecticut River Valley. Like the Abenakis near Lake Champlain, they had villages in the warmer, more fertile intervale areas and hunted, gathered and farmed. During the

A fragment of prehistory, this bit of pottery was part of a vessel used by the
Abenakis to store or cook food. It was excavated from a site near Newbury.

warm months of the year, the Abenakis lived in their villages, but late in the year, all but the aged and infirm would move to their winter hunting grounds, which were located in upland, hilly areas. Each band had its own roughly delineated hunting ground to which it returned, year after year.

Scholars estimate that each major band had about 500 people, which is in line with other hunting and gathering societies worldwide. They believe that a total of about 2,000 people lived in the four villages near the shores of Lake Champlain, while another 1,000 or so lived in the Connecticut River Valley.

Their society appears to have been a successful one. It was egalitarian and not aggressively warlike, like the Iroquois to the west. They made pots and baskets, traded with other native peoples over far-flung trade routes, and from time to time conducted elaborate burial ceremonies.

"At the beginning of the seventeenth century Western Abenakis probably ate better, had a slightly longer life expectancy, more leisure time, and experienced less violence in their lives than people living in Europe," anthropologist Haviland has written.

The arrival of Europeans in Vermont in the seventeenth and eighteenth centuries immediately threatened the established Indian ways of life. Not only were they decimated by European diseases to which they had no immunity, they were exploited by the newcomers in the fur trade and in a series of frontier conflicts between French and English known as the French and Indian Wars.

As English settlers moved from the south into what would later become Vermont and the surrounding territory, the French were moving down from the north. The Abenakis sided with the French for a variety of reasons, including the accounts they had heard of English brutality to Native Americans in southern New England. The result was a dramatic series of Indian raids on English settlements in the seventeenth and eighteenth centuries. Once captured, English settlers would then be marched back into French Canada and held for ransom. Records suggest that 1,196 English settlers were taken to Canada during that time. Perhaps the most famous raid by the Abenakis was the Deerfield Massacre of 1704 in nearby Deerfield, Mass. Much of the population of early Deerfield was killed or captured and marched northward to Canada by French-led Abenakis.

In the last days of the French and Indian Wars, a young major named Robert Rogers came to fight for the British, who were beginning to experiment with tactics that were frankly genocidal. Ordered to wipe out an Abenaki village on the St. Francis River, Rogers attacked and killed about 30 people before struggling back to the English frontier through the wilderness. Although his exploits were later glorified and Rogers claimed 200 victims, many modern historians consider his attack a bloody failure that was unnecessary.

After the close of the French and Indian War with the Treaty of Paris in 1763, the history of the Abenakis becomes splintered and obscure until modern times. But beginning in 1976, descendants of the Abenakis in Swanton began to speak out for themselves and demand recognition and rights. They have formed the Abenaki Self-Help Association, the Abenaki Tribal Council, and have asked for fishing and hunting rights, as well as federal recognition of their tribal status. Although recognized in Canada, the Abenakis have yet to gain recognition from the State of Vermont.

LAKE CHAMPLAIN

L ake Champlain dominates much of western Vermont and has had at least as profound an impact on the state's history and culture as the mountains that gave Vermont its nickname.

After the Great Lakes, Champlain is the largest freshwater lake in the United States. It is 109 miles long and 11 miles wide at its widest, and occupies a 20-mile-wide valley that contains much of the best farm land in Vermont and Burlington, the largest city, which, with its several satellite communities is home to roughly a fifth of the state's population of about one-half million.

Geologically, the lake is the center of an immense glacial valley that was once an inland arm of the Atlantic Ocean. The present lake, though small in comparison to its prehistoric form, is a major recreation center, and was an important factor in the early history of both Vermont and the United States.

Samuel de Champlain discovered the lake in 1609, and its long and remarkable history began with a century of exploration by both French and English. Author Ralph Nading Hill of Burlington has called the lake "the most historic body of water in the western hemisphere," and goes on to say eloquently why that is so. In colonial times, Hill writes in his book, *Lake Champlain, Key to Liberty*, the lake was "a silver dagger from Canada to the heartland of the American colonies." To use a humbler metaphor, the big lake could be called an interstate highway of the eighteenth century, because travel in those days was much easier via water than through the largely untracked land. Whoever controlled the waters of Champlain had dominion over a broad, navigable thoroughfare that split New England from the rest of the colonies and linked Canada with the Hudson River Valley and ultimately New York City.

In that context, it is easy to see why Fort Ticonderoga, overlooking the narrows of Lake Champlain at the outlet of Lake George, in New York State, was a strategic focus of the lake's early history. The Revolutionary War battles of Bennington and Hubbardton, and the subsequent defeat of the British at nearby Saratoga, N.Y., were all related to the

A battleground no more, Lake Champlain sparkles in the sunshine off North Hero.

British attempt to capture the Champlain Valley. The lake also figured, though to a lesser extent, in the War of 1812, and it had a vigorous commercial history during the steamboating era of the nineteenth century. The last of the lake's great steam boats, the Ticonderoga, can be seen and toured at Shelburne Museum, a few minutes drive from the lake's shores.

Evidence of Champlain's lengthy past can be seen at historic sites up and down the lake and, for those with diving skills, at Vermont's only underwater state parks, three preserves located and marked for scuba divers in Burlington Bay. Each of the preserves—the *General Butler* Underwater Historic Preserve, the *Phoenix* Underwater Preserve, and the Coal Barge Underwater Preserve—allows divers access to a historic shipwreck, naturally preserved for many years by the lake's cold waters.

There are a variety of other historic sites on both sides of the lake. These are some located in Vermont:

- **St. Anne's Shrine, Isle La Motte.** The picturesque Roman Catholic shrine is on the site of Fort St. Anne, the first white settlement in Vermont. The fort was constructed in 1666.
- **Hyde Log Cabin, Grand Isle.** Considered the oldest log cabin in the U.S., it is furnished with eighteenth and nineteenth century furniture and is open from July through Labor Day.
- **Shelburne Farms.** Located on one of the most beautiful waterfront settings in Vermont, this 3,800-acre nineteenth century "duchy" of the Webb family is Vermont's grandest estate, and one of the finest in New England. The buildings and barns are now used as an educational and cultural center and are open from June through September for tours and special events. The main house is to become an inn.
- **Shelburne Museum.** An amazing museum of museums in which is gathered one of the finest collections of Americana in the U.S., fine paintings, and much cultural and historical material from the Champlain Valley region. Open mid-May through mid-October and at Christmas and other special times during the year.

- **The Winooski Falls Historic District.** Textile mills were first established in the village of Winooski in 1835, and operated there, in one instance, until 1954. The mill buildings have been rehabilitated and provide offices, condominiums, and retail space, helping to revitalize the small city just north of Burlington.
- **Chimney Point Tavern, Addison.** For nearly 100 years, this eighteenth century structure served as an inn. Legend holds that in its taproom, Ethan Allen was once surprised by the British and narrowly escaped capture. Now it is a small museum, open mid-May to mid-October. Closed Mondays and Tuesdays.
- **Mount Independence, Orwell.** A fort built here was occupied by units of the Continental Army during the Revolution. Remains of the star-shaped fort, hospital, blockhouses, gun batteries, and three miles of trails in a rural setting are included in this national historic landmark, which is located north of Chipman's Point, opposite Fort Ticonderoga in New York State.
- **The Hubbardton Battlefield.** The site of the only Revolutionary War battle actually waged on Vermont soil, where American rebels fought a rear-guard action that slowed the British and may have contributed to the subsequent American victory at Bennington.
- **The John Strong DAR Mansion, West Addison.** Built in 1796, the house has a beautifully designed entrance and contains many items of interest, including an artfully concealed hiding place in its massive chimney. Open May 15-Oct. 15, admission is charged.
- **The Basin Harbor Maritime Museum, Vergennes.** Housed in an 1888 stone schoolhouse, the collection traces Lake Champlain's history from its earliest geologic beginnings to the present day. Adjacent to one of the lake's oldest and most elegant resorts, it is open daily or by appointment.

ETHAN ALLEN AND THE GREEN MOUNTAIN BOYS

T o understand the loud-mouthed, brawling, larger-than-life character named Ethan Allen, one must remember that the country that later became Vermont was, in the late 1700s, still a frontier, where rules were few and fortune went to those bold enough to claim it. Whatever else Ethan Allen may have been, he was bold. His size, his physical strength, his intelligence and his astonishing powers of invective helped him become the dominant public figure in Vermont's formative years. But it was his boldness that made him great.

He, along with his younger, craftier brother, Ira, and several other relatives, came to Vermont from Connecticut in the 1760s to make their fortunes. They immediately began buying and speculating in land under grants made in the region by Benning Wentworth, the colonial governor of New Hampshire. But there was a problem. New York authorities did not recognize New Hampshire's authority to make grants in the area and instead issued their own. The result was a confusion of claims and counter-claims over who actually owned land in Vermont.

Ethan Allen emerged early in the dispute as a spokesman for the speculators and settlers who held title to their land under grants from New Hampshire. The Green Mountain Boys, later to win fame in the Revolutionary War, were first organized in and around Bennington as an irregular defense committee to defend the recognition of New Hampshire grants against New York authority. Naturally (given his personality) Allen assumed the role of leader and the title of "colonel-commander." The New York authorities were well aware of the Green Mountain Boys, but thought of them considerably less heroically. They referred to the group as "the Bennington Mob." But after a 20-year struggle, the Hampshire grant-holders and the Allens triumphed and it is as the Green Mountain Boys that they are remembered today.

Allen's most spectacular triumph—the capture of Fort Ticonderoga—came in 1775. Inspired by the battles of Concord and Lexington, Allen immediately saw the strategic significance of the great stone fortress overlooking the narrows of Lake Champlain. He also knew the fort was decrepit, and manned by a small garrison. He was already plotting its capture when Gen. Benedict Arnold arrived in Vermont with orders to capture the fort. Fortunately for Allen, his Green Mountain Boys refused to follow

Fred G. Hill

Ethan Allen's last homestead, located in
the Burlington Intervale (inset: the
building's interior).

Arnold, whose own troops had not yet caught up to him, and rallied behind their longtime leader. In the early-morning hours of May 10, 1775, Allen, Arnold and a handful of the Green Mountain Boys crossed the lake, slipped into the all but unguarded fort, and forced its surrender without killing a single person. Allen later declared that he had demanded the fort "in the name of the Continental Congress and the Great Jehovah," but his contemporaries say he actually shouted something like, "Come out of there, you damned old rat!" In any case, he lost no time in notifying authorities of his triumph and reaping proper recognition.

That triumph was followed later that same year by Allen's most spectacular fiasco—his botched attack on the City of Montreal and his own subsequent capture by the British. He was confined in English prisons for more than two years.

After that, his influence was never the same, partially because he lost the limelight, but mostly because, as historian Charles Jellison has noted, Vermont had changed. No longer frontier, it had become a more settled, farmed, orderly realm that had little use for loud-talking, unpredictable heroes.

Allen flirted briefly with British authorities in Canada, hinting that he might help return Vermont to British authority, but nothing ever came of it. The Revolution finally ended with Vermont on its way to statehood, although that goal was not attained for several years, and for 14 years Vermont existed as an independent republic.

The old hero's final years were spent in uncharacteristic quiet at his farm on the Intervale of the Winooski River near Burlington. The farm and Allen's home are being restored and the grounds are open to the public. He died there on Feb. 12, 1789, aged 51, after a drinking bout in South Hero with his cousin, Ebeneezer Allen. Vermont has never forgotten him, and a statue of him may be seen on the State House steps in Montpelier. Like much of the Allen legend, his statue is based on guess and hearsay since no one now knows for certain just what Vermont's boldest hero actually looked like.

MONTPELIER, AMERICA'S SMALLEST CAPITAL

A trip through the Vermont State House is a good introduction to Vermont and the Vermont ethic, for the building shares many characteristics of the state it symbolizes. It is small, beautiful, has a long and intricate history, and displays the Yankee virtues of thrift and simplicity, with a touch of understated, granite-bound elegance.

In the early 1800s Montpelier might have been thought one of the towns least likely to be chosen Vermont's capital. At that time the larger cities were in the southern part of the state, and the legislature had bounced from town to town, alternating for a time between the east and west sides of the Green Mountains.

But Montpelier was near the geographic center of the state, and since it was not involved in the fervent competition among other cities (such as Windsor and Rutland) to be the seat of Vermont's new state government, it emerged as a compromise location. It didn't hurt that the city's civic leaders had pledged $8,000 toward the building of a State House (roughly half its cost). In 1805, Montpelier was chosen, and by 1808, the first State House, a strange rectangular wooden building with a belfry and recessed front porches, was constructed. It later became dilapidated and over-crowded—one historian said the Yankee penchant for whittling had produced large holes in the members' desks—and a new building was planned. Designed by architect Ammi B. Young after the Greek temple of Theseus, it was built in 1838 and destroyed by fire when a woodstove exploded one cold January night in 1857. Its granite columns and portico were saved, however, and incorporated into the third and present State House, which was dedicated in 1859 and has been in regular use ever since as the home of the Vermont legislature.

The building has chambers for the House and Senate plus ceremonial offices for the governor and lieutenant governor. It is a repository of Vermont history and tradition (as is the Vermont Historical Society Museum in the Pavilion Building nearby) with a significant collection of Civil War memorabilia and historic Vermont paintings, including the heroic-sized "Battle of Cedar Creek," by Julian Scott, which depicts the Vermont Brigade entering the 1864 battle of the same name. The painting covers one wall in a large reception room dubbed "The War Room" by the State House press corps.

There is a massive statue of Vermont hero Ethan Allen on the portico outside the front door of the building and a hand-carved allegorical figure symbolizing "Agriculture" decorates the top of the golden dome. It is a piece of genuine folk art, carved in 1938 by former Sgt.-at-Arms Dwight Dwinnell, and replaced an earlier statue, which had deteriorated.

Lesser-known features of the venerable building include the so-called "Aiken window," where former Gov. (later U.S. Sen.) George D. Aiken would slip into the building late at night when he had forgotten his key. A mark on the left front gatepost, adjacent to State Street, indicates the high-water mark of the Winooski River in the state's greatest catastrophe, the Flood of 1927.

In the Hall of Inscriptions, just off the lower lobby, some of the state's spirit is captured in quotations painted on the walls. This one from the writings of Thomas Chittenden, Vermont's first governor, is characteristic:

> Out of storm and manifold perils rose an
> enduring state, the home of freedom and unity.

Near the State House are several other interesting buildings, perhaps most notably the Pavilion Office Building, which houses the Vermont Historical Society, the governor's offices, and several other state agencies and departments. The Pavilion looks old, but was actually built in 1970, a reconstruction of the elegant old Pavilion Hotel, which stood on the site until it was demolished in 1969.

Montpelier, a quiet attractive city of about 8,000 inhabitants, has its share of fine buildings, parades and festivals. But most notably, it has gained a measure of attention in recent years for its size: it is the smallest state capital in the U.S. The distinction seems quite fitting.

The gold-domed, granite State House nestles snugly against a wooded Montpelier hillside. Here, the state symphony plays.

VERMONT'S DISTINCTIVE ARCHITECTURE

A lthough Vermont is primarily known for its natural beauty, humanity has shaped the land and its appearance since the earliest days. The "built landscape" of barns, churches, villages, and covered bridges is both a readable historic record of the past and an architectural patchwork of considerable beauty.

COVERED BRIDGES

Some structures, such as covered bridges, have the status of sacred relics. They are preserved and treasured; their loss is mourned, and communities often rebuild them at considerable expense if they are destroyed. Although they are surely less utilitarian than a modern concrete structure, they just as surely have more character.

Because they are made of wood, covered bridges are vulnerable to floods and fires. But there are still many of them around. To see a lot of them in one trip, go to North Bennington, which has three, or Northfield, which has five, or the Montgomery-Berkshire area, which has seven, or the Johnson-Waterville area, which has eight. To see what is believed to be the oldest covered bridge in Vermont, go to Middlebury and find the Pulpmill Covered Bridge, a Burr arch truss bridge built across Otter Creek around 1820 that has a rare two-lane design.

Why were covered bridges covered? Not to keep the snow out, as many people suppose. Actually, snow was shoveled *into* covered bridges in pre-automobile days, for the sleighs. The bridges were covered for maintenance purposes to keep the harsh northern wind and weather off their timbers.

BARNS

The classic pastoral landscape looks, at first glance, much as it did 100 years ago. But in recent years, subtle changes have occurred that are quite evident to the knowing eye. For one thing, there's less landscape that's visible nowadays. Vermont was mostly open fields a century or even three-quarters of a century ago; now it's mostly forested.

Barns are different now, too. The classic red barn of 50 years ago has become an endangered species, as has its cylindrical wooden silo. Contemporary barns often look

The human landscape: Waits River's quiet elegance offers proportion, restraint.

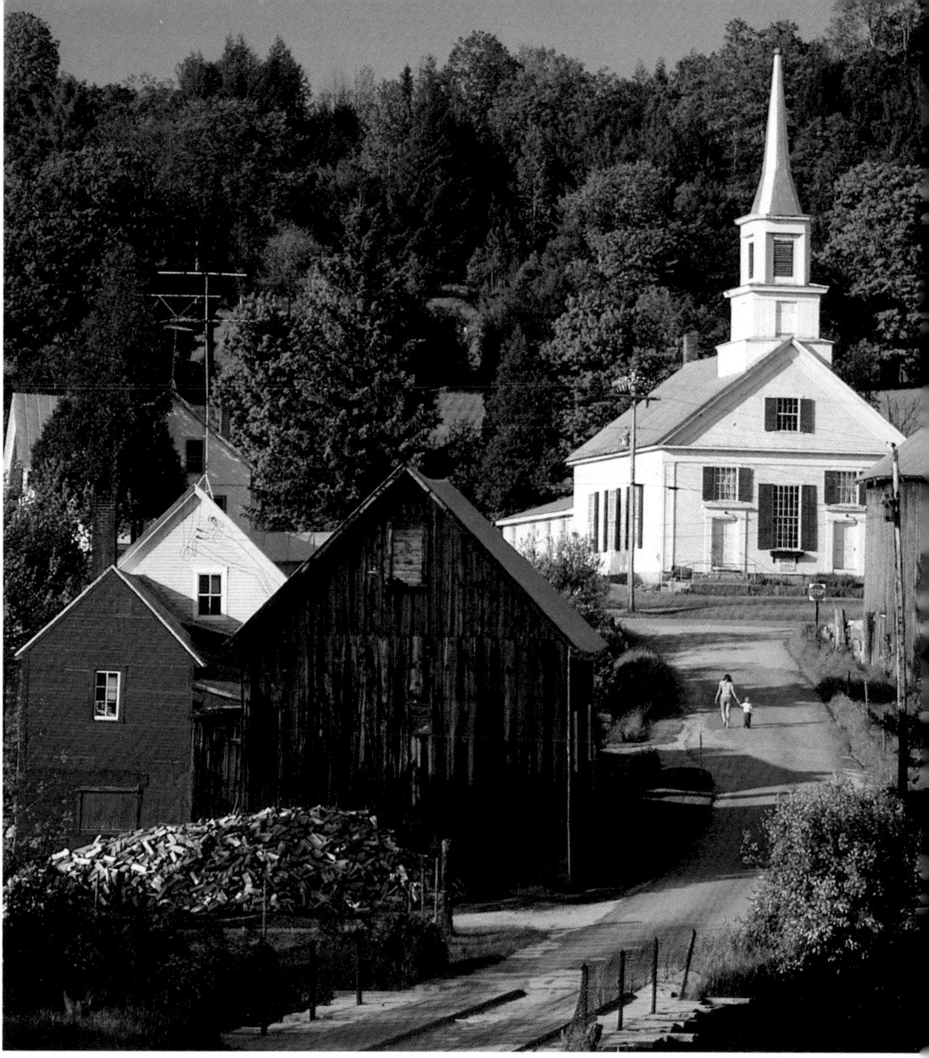

Marilyn S. Rogers

like glorified sheds or outsized metal quonset huts. Silos these days are often concrete-lined troughs bulldozed horizontally into the earth and covered with plastic film, or those immense, blue, sealed thermos bottles that cost thousands of dollars and are used to store a new form of grass-feed for cows called "haylage." The most picturesque old barns are now sometimes unusable—either too small or poorly configured—for a modern dairy operation, which depends upon complex feeding systems and milking "parlors." However, some farmers have refurbished their old wooden barns simply because they like the traditional appearance. For the experienced farmland-watcher, there's a rule of thumb for gauging whether an old farm is prospering or not: check out the barn. If it has been enlarged, updated or replaced, the farm is probably doing well.

CHURCHES

That principle is less reliable as a guide to churches. Several Vermont churches built in the 1700s and early 1800s still hoist their white spires to the sky, and most of those that still exist are in good repair. They are like time machines. Simply to enter the Strafford or Rockingham meeting houses, Old Bennington's First Congregational Church, the Middlebury Congregational Church, the Old West Church in Calais, or any of a dozen other such buildings, to stand in the clear, eloquent light of their finely proportioned interiors, and to sense the restraint, care and order that went into their construction is to learn volumes about the faith of our fathers. However, many of the very old buildings are now owned and maintained as a historical resource by the town in which they are located and no longer house a congregation. This is true, for example, of Richmond's Old Round Church, easily Vermont's most unusual church (and one of its most beautiful), which is maintained by the Richmond Historical Society.

Others are still used for worship. The tiny, charming Starksboro Meeting House, after some years of disuse, has been restored and put to use by a local meeting of the Religious Society of Friends (Quakers), the sect that originally built it.

VILLAGES

Vermont's cities and villages are architectural treasure troves, often containing 200 years worth of architectural styles in churches, public buildings, and private homes. Architecture-watching is one of Vermont's secret delights. The elegance, whimsy, pomposity, beauty, even humor of past ages can be glimpsed in many of the buildings we walk past every day. For a preliminary tour, here are some rewarding villages to visit, and some buildings not to miss.

- **St. Johnsbury.** A fine collection of grand old buildings, mostly of late nineteenth century vintage. The Athenaeum and the Fairbanks Museum, both gifts of the Fairbanks family, are outstanding.
- **St. Albans.** Especially the monumental row of public buildings on the east side of Taylor Park, downtown.
- **Stowe.** The Greek Revival Helen Day Memorial Library and Art Center, the elegantly thin-spired Stowe Community Church, and several fine homes are notable.
- **Middlebury.** This mill village with a college boasts nearly 300 buildings from the eighteenth and nineteenth centuries, including the Congregational Church mentioned above.
- **Chelsea.** With two beautiful commons and many well-preserved buildings, Chelsea retains the appearance of an early nineteenth century village. The Orange County Court House is a Greek Revival classic.
- **Castleton.** Despite the busy highway through its center, Castleton maintains the quiet charm of an earlier day. Several outstanding Federal style residences are here.
- **Dorset.** Green-shuttered white buildings arranged around an oval commons. One of the prettiest (and richest) villages in Vermont.
- **Manchester Village.** Home of Vermont's grandest inn, The Equinox, and one of the finest mansions, Robert Todd Lincoln's Hildene.
- **Newfane.** Lovely asymmetrical green surrounded by significant nineteenth century buildings.
- **Old Bennington.** The beautiful church mentioned above is but one of many in this beautiful hilltop neighborhood. Despite the bustle of modern-day Bennington nearby, it still feels as though Ethan Allen might come walking down the street at any moment.

THE PASTORAL LANDSCAPE

V ermont's beauty stands out in all New England because it is farmed. Although its mountains are lovely, they are not as spectacular as the Adirondacks or the White Mountains. But Vermont is, to many people, more beautiful than either upstate New York or New Hampshire, and the principal difference is that Vermont retains a "working rural landscape" — its farm land.

That is something of a reversal of the fashion of 100 years ago, when the Adirondack and White Mountain regions were both more popular as tourist destinations than Vermont. In the mid-1800s, travelers commonly sought vistas that were "sublime" — that is, grand and wild. Vermont, a farmed land of thoroughly tamed pastoral views, lacked sublimity. But around the turn of the century, city-weary travelers began to seek pastoral retreats and pure wilderness lost much of its drawing power.

Why has Vermont been farmed so intensively for so long? Both geology and sociology provide a part of the answer. Vermont's soils are less acidic than the granitic mountain soils of upstate New Hampshire and New York, and it has regions of great fertility in the Champlain Valley, the northern river valleys, and the eastern Piedmont sections. Also, Vermont was settled by people intent on holding their land independently, and the best way to do that 200 years ago was by farming. Therefore, Vermonters had both the motivation and the land needed to make farming work, and farm they did. Known as the "breadbasket of New England" 150 years ago, Vermont is still New England's leading dairy state.

For that reason, more of the great forest that once covered all of the Northeast and continually tries to re-cover the region has been kept at bay. The valleys seem broader and more open; the mountains are more visible. And the patchwork interplay of meadowland, forest, mountains and small villages that typifies so much of the Vermont countryside creates a landscape that is idyllic and pastoral, one that reminds nearly everyone of the good things rural life stands for.

However, while there are many nostalgic ideas associated with farming, and everyone favors the family farm in theory, it is a rugged and demanding life. A variety of

In the springtime meadows of Tunbridge, the year begins again.

economic problems have recently pummeled farmers in Vermont as elsewhere in the United States. Over-production of milk means that dairy farmers are losing the battle of supply and demand. At the same time, cleared farm land is attractive to real estate developers. Some farmers are deciding to sell their herds and their land. Also, it is very difficult for new, young farmers to find the $250,000 to $600,000 needed to start a full-scale dairy operation.

Only about 19 percent of Vermont is now being farmed, and the 3,000 or so dairy farms in Vermont are decreasing by about 60 per year. Vermonters now cultivate and pasture only about half the land they used in 1950.

Vermonters are doing their best to keep the family farm alive here because they realize its value to both the Vermont landscape and the Vermont heritage. Gov. Madeleine M. Kunin told a group in Brattleboro in 1986:

> When I stop and think about some of the values for which Vermont is noted today—a strong work ethic, honesty, independence—I conclude that these qualities are directly related to our agricultural heritage. We are not an agricultural society, yet we hold on to these ways. These values that create a bond with the land, a respect for the natural environment, a sense of community, and a respect for individuality—these are the values that distinguish us from the rest of America.

DAIRY FARMS

M ost Vermont farmers are dairy farmers, because "making milk" has long been the surest way to produce an income from this land. Although Vermont farmers also raise sheep and beef, grow apples, grain, and vegetables, dairy income now makes up 90 percent of all Vermont farm income, and is worth about $340 million per year.

Because of its cool, moist weather, Vermont grows grass crops—hay—supremely well. Major New England cities give Vermont farmers a ready-made market. Once an exporter of meat and grain, Vermont focused on dairying when the broad ranges of the Midwest and West pushed the Green Mountain State's hilly pastures (which are snow-covered four to five months of each year) out of the sheep business before the Civil War. Meat can be shipped in to the cities from the Midwest, or even from New Zealand, but fresh milk must be produced close by. Federal milk-marketing orders in recent years have sent most of Vermont's milk into Boston and southern New England, and Vermont now supplies about 40 percent of the milk New England drinks.

Not all cows are created equal, and farmers choose different breeds for a variety of reasons, some economic, some personal.

Holsteins, the black-and-white cows that dot hillsides throughout the state during the warm months, are the most popular breed because they produce so much milk. Through selective breeding and special feeding programs, a single Holstein can produce nearly 25,000 pounds of milk in a year (although most produce less).

Many Vermont farmers, however, prefer Jerseys, which are smaller, gentler cows that produce creamier milk, though less of it. Jerseys are commonly a tawny, light-brown color, and they have dark, almost liquid eyes; their calves seem as delicate as fawns. Some Vermont dairymen keep Ayrshires or Guernseys, smaller brown or reddish-brown and white cattle regarded as highly efficient milk producers. A few herds of Brown Swiss cattle can also be found in Vermont. One such herd at Shelburne Farms produces milk for a superb cheddar cheese. Top production figures for all those breeds reach 20,000 pounds of milk annually per cow.

More and more in recent years, part-time or hobby farmers have chosen to raise beef cattle such as Herefords, Black Angus, Charolais or shaggy Scotch Highland cattle.

Although some dairymen look down on hobby farmers, most authorities agree that as dairying faces increasing problems in the years ahead, Vermont's agricultural future depends, to some extent, on the success of its part-time farmers.

Nearly everyone who stays with farming does so because he or she loves it. Although it is a hard life, it has many rewards, which range from being one's own boss to living close to nature and working with living things every day. Walter Smith, a Plainfield farmer, spoke for many of his fellows when he told an interviewer recently:

> I worked like hang for my farm, and that farm has more value for me than I could ever get for it and put in the bank. . . . I don't want it sold out of the family. If you've worked all your life for something, you want to hang right on to it to the bitter end—and be sure the bitter end doesn't come too soon.

Daniel A. Neary, Jr.

**Sunlight dapples cattle, barn, and the flank of the Worcester Range in this
East Montpelier view.**

WINTER'S RIGORS

F rom December through March, the essential fact of life in Vermont is winter. Preparations for it often occupy so much of the rest of the year that Vermont's short, intensely beautiful summers can seem to be little more than a respite.

The coldest month of winter is January, when temperatures often fall below freezing for weeks and below zero for several days at a time. January averages 17°, according to the U.S. Weather Service in Burlington. But averages do not convey the truth of what a winter in Vermont is like. It brings the reality a little closer when it is noted that the coldest temperature ever recorded in the state was -50°, at Bloomfield, in northeastern Vermont, on December 30, 1933. (Bloomfield, incidentally, is Vermont's coldest town. It has set six of the 12 all-time low monthly temperature readings.) In Burlington, where Lake Champlain moderates the temperatures a bit, the coldest ever recorded is -30°, recorded twice, in 1957 and 1979.

There are many unofficial readings even colder. In the high mountain valleys of the Northeast Kingdom, there is often talk of readings as low as -60°. And though that is not close on the world-scale of record cold (Siberia: -90°; Antarctica: -126°), it is certainly cold enough, and four to five months of freezing weather and snowstorms is long enough.

Vermont usually gets a total of more than five feet of snow per winter, but since much of it settles and melts between snowstorms, ordinarily there may be only a foot or so on the ground, except in the mountains, where there may be far more. Actually, snow cover varies greatly. Often there may be two feet of snow in Montpelier, a few inches in Bennington, and none in Burlington.

Statistically, the snowiest month in Vermont is March, and the greatest snowfall in Vermont history occurred over a three-day period in March of 1947, in the southern Vermont town of Readsboro. Four feet, two inches of snow fell.

Everyone can tell snowstorm stories, but surprisingly few Vermonters have actually frozen to death. Writer Charles Edward Crane said he knew of only one, and

Winter's stern reality is tempered with much beauty, as here in Lower Waterford.

that death had occurred in 1821, when the wife of one Harrison Blake died when Blake tried to drive his sleigh over Stratton Mountain to Arlington at the height of a blizzard.

Blake made it to within two miles of a tavern near the present-day mountain village of Kelly Stand when his horse could go no further because of the snow. Blake wrapped his wife and infant daughter in his overcoat and struggled off through the storm, desperately hoping to reach help at the tavern. But he sank exhausted into the snow. He was found alive the next morning, and told his rescuers to push on. They found Mrs. Blake dying. She perished before she could be removed from the mountain. But the baby, wrapped in the overcoat and some of her mother's clothing, survived.

Popular balladeers of the day retold the story as verse and it has since passed into Vermont legend. The last two verses can still inspire a shiver, even in July:

She took the mantle from her breast
And bared her bosom to the storm.
As round the child she wrapped the vest,
She smiled to think that it was warm.
One cold kiss, one tear she shed,
And sank upon the snowy bed.

A traveler passing by next morn
Saw her neath the snowy veil.
The frost of death was in her eye;
Her cheek was hard and cold and pale.
He took the robe from off the child;
The babe looked up and sweetly smiled.

Less poetically, even a modern winter bares the hard edge of necessity for everyone who lives here year-round. Whether it is a matter of getting the car started and going to work, or keeping the house warm and tight, it is difficult at -20°. The season is hardest on the poor, the elderly, and on those who must work outdoors.

And yet it transforms the world in ways that are not completely unpleasant. A week of December's -10° banishes November's slush and slime, covers the rivers with ice and the streamside trees with hoarfrost. If life becomes more difficult and taxing, it can also be more husbanded, more focused.

Spring is hope and summer is ambrosia. But winter, with its piles of wood, its hot stoves, its mulled cider, and its hard, clear purity of cold night and colder stars—winter is reality. It is hard not to love it, even as we curse it.

SKIING IN VERMONT

T here are fashions in recreation, just as there are in clothing. A century ago, people came to Vermont to "take the waters" at mineral springs in Highgate, Manchester, Clarendon and elsewhere. Today the largest single recreational drawing card is skiing, which directly adds more than $275 million to the Vermont economy. In the 1985–86 season, about 1.5 million people bought 4.5 million lift tickets. Skiing has transformed Vermont's winters—and some of its landscape—in a half century.

Skiing was popularized here in the 1930s and 1940s by pioneers like Bromley Mountain's Fred Pabst and Stowe's Sepp Ruschp. The first recorded ascent of Mount Mansfield on skis is believed to have occurred in 1914. But modern-day, lift-assisted skiing wasn't born in Stowe or Stratton or Manchester; it began on farmer Clinton Gilbert's hillside cow pasture just north of Woodstock. It was there in 1934 that a Model T Ford engine was hooked up to some pulleys and a rope to become the first ski tow in the United States. The next year there was a ski lift in operation at Bunny Bertram's Suicide Six area nearby.

Skiing very quickly generated a tremendous amount of excitement and within the next few years, new ski trails and ski tows began cropping up all over northern New England. By 1937 there were four ski areas with lifts in Vermont—at Bromley Mountain near Manchester, Pico Peak near Rutland, Suicide Six, and Mount Mansfield in Stowe. The famous "Skimeister" ski trains began bringing skiers to Waterbury, just south of Stowe, in 1935, two years before the first rope tow appeared on Mount Mansfield. In 1940, the Mount Mansfield Co. installed the state's first chairlift.

In the early days, skiers who came by train sometimes found themselves stranded without transportation in the frosty pre-dawn hours. Lodgings were often a farmhouse or a rustic and hastily improvised inn, and warming huts were few and far between. Most mountains had to be climbed on skis before they could be skied down: it was a sport for the young and rugged. However, with the post-World War II recreation explosion, Vermont skiing expanded dramatically. The State of Vermont encouraged that expansion by building access roads and clearing legal and procedural roadblocks. Killington, Mount Snow, Sugarbush and other giants of the modern ski trade were created in the major ski expansion of the 1950s and 1960s.

The rise in popularity of cross-country skiing has done nothing to quell the growth of downhill skiing. Rather, it has added a new realm of wintertime activity, and many skiers enjoy both. Vermont's first public cross-country ski touring center was opened at the Trapp Family Lodge in Stowe in 1967. Today there are more than 50.

For many years Vermont has produced world-class Alpine ski racers, among them Olympic champions Andrea Mead Lawrence, Billy Kidd and Barbara Cochran. The state has also dominated America's less successful efforts to break into the top class of international Nordic (cross-country) racers. Mike Gallagher, Bob Gray, Martha Rockwell and Tim Caldwell led U.S. Nordic skiing for some time, but it was a Putney youth, Bill Koch, who was the first American to win an Olympic Nordic skiing medal. Koch was also the first American to win a World Cup in the sport.

The fact that skiing is recreational does not make it an inconsequential activity— far from it. In addition to generating millions of dollars in economic activity annually and contributing about $16 million in taxes on sales, rooms and meals, it has transformed Vermont socially and economically in the span of a single lifetime. Mountain towns, such as Stratton, that were isolated and impoverished 40 years ago have been revitalized and are now among the state's wealthiest. Less obvious has been the occasional social dislocation that has at times pitted wealthy newcomer against low-income native Vermonter, causing resentment on both sides.

Such dislocations, though they raise questions about the future of the state, are to be expected in a socio-economic revolution as profound as that which skiing, an obscure sport hardly known outside Scandinavia 75 years ago, has brought to the Green Mountains.

Clyde H. Smith

A cold, sunny morning, a foot of new powder, the trail all to oneself— perfection!
(Here experienced at Sugarbush Ski Area in Warren).

THE SUGAR MAPLE TREE

T he late U.S. Sen. George D. Aiken once called maple trees Vermont's "lovely loafers," because so many of them were untapped—unproductive and therefore idle in the view of Vermont's longtime farmer-senator.

The demand for maple syrup, the emergence of new technology, and the research done in recent years at the University of Vermont's maple research center have begun to change that perception. In any case, it is characteristic that Vermont's state tree is the sugar maple, *Acer saccharum*, a species that is both beautiful and immensely practical, offering a cash reward, maple syrup and the springtime elixir of vigorous outdoor work.

The maple season is an annual ritual that marks the end of winter and looks toward "mud season" and the real spring to come. Like many Vermont pastimes, it is fun with a distinctly practical side—or perhaps it would be more accurate to say that it is work, but work that is not total drudgery.

The first European settlers learned sugaring from the native Abenakis and in the frontier years boiled maple sap in open kettles over bonfires until it crystalized into maple sugar for their tables. Nowadays, comparatively little sugar is made. Most of the sap is used for syrup, and its making can be a complex science often involving ultraviolet lights, pre-evaporation, hydrometer tests, and miles and miles of plastic tubing. Sugaring has changed considerably from the days when the Indians simply gashed a tree's bark with an axe to collect sap. Even the metal buckets used nearly universally 30 years ago have been replaced in many sugaring operations by plastic tubes and collecting pumps called "sapsuckers."

Far from being a subsistence sweetener, today's maple syrup now sells for more than $20 a gallon. Syrup is graded by its color, which ranges from "fancy" (the lightest in color and most delicate in taste) through several grades of amber. Though the lowest grades are dark and best used for cooking, many Vermont residents prefer the stronger maple taste and darker color of a "Grade A medium amber" or "dark amber." Sugar-making is still a very individualized art that depends on the skill and care of the sugarmaker and the quality of sap used. Old-time sugarmakers can tell by taste which

Paul O. Boisvert

Sugaring: Turning winter into spring by dint of effort. A blustery day for sap gathering in Orange.

hillside or sugarbush has produced a given barrel of syrup, much as a skilled winemaker can locate, by taste and bouquet, the vineyard that produced a bottle of wine.

Maple syrup is now a big business, worth $11 million to Vermont maple producers in 1985. Vermont remains the leading producer of maple syrup in the U.S., with 495,000 gallons in 1983 and 530,000 gallons in 1984. The Vermont maple crop is increasing, according to the state Agriculture Department, largely because more trees are being tapped and higher yields are being obtained per tap. An exception to this trend was in 1986, when bad sugaring weather (sugaring needs chilly nights and warm, clear days) played hob with the plans of Vermont maple producers.

Despite the economic pressures and technological changes of modern sugar-making, some things remain the same. Although there is an immense amount of work involved, most farmers still look forward to the sugaring season because it offers them a chance to be outdoors and active in the exuberant days of early spring. After a long, confining winter, sugaring's rush of activity is greeted happily, as is the cash bonus involved. There are very few places where springtime's goodness is more strongly affirmed than in the sweet-smelling, steamy interior of an April sugarhouse. The fire's warmth, the misty perfume of boiling sap, and the awakening life of the world outside make the days seem as full of hope and anticipation as any in the year.

Few sugarmakers begrudge the long hours of labor gathering sap and tending the boiling pan, and many of them welcome visitors. For a list of sugarhouses where sugaring can be observed each spring, call or write the Vermont Department of Agriculture, 116 State St., Montpelier, Vt. 05602; telephone 802–828–2500.

FOREST WEALTH

Dense forests blanketed Vermont in a nearly impenetrable tangle when the state was being—almost literally—hacked from the wilderness. The first settlers had to work like demons to clear the land, and in many cases detested the dark woods that surrounded them. They had good reason. Forests were wild, dangerous places, and a leading cause of male deaths in the early years of many Vermont towns was falling trees.

Today Vermont forests are regarded as a resource, not a threat. They are a source of building material, a place for rest and recreation. And most significantly in the past decade, they have emerged as a source of home-grown energy.

Wood, says the commonplace, is the fuel that warms you twice, once when you cut it, and once again when it's burned. In fact, if a person were to do all the work needed to get a winter's supply of wood from forest to stove, it would heat them at least a dozen times: cutting, hauling, splitting, stacking, unstacking, and hand-feeding several cords of wood each winter to a stove or furnace is a prodigious amount of physical labor. Yet many Vermonters became wood-choppers during the years of the energy crisis and today just under half the homes in Vermont are heated with wood, either partially or completely.

It took the energy crisis of the early 1970s to convince Vermonters that they should re-learn the wood-burning skills of their grandparents. Vermont's collective sense of independence and self-reliance was burnished to a bright, slightly self-righteous glow when the state survived those cold, energy-thin winters by dint of a traditional technology—wood-burning—and a lot of hard work. The state Public Service Department estimates that Vermonters now save about 450,000 gallons of fuel oil each winter by burning wood.

Also during those years, Vermonters proved they are still an ingenious bunch, inventing and marketing a dozen or more new designs for woodstoves. One of those designs, the Defiant by Vermont Castings in Randolph, became a symbol of the return to wood-fired independence and triumphed as a national best-seller.

The use of heating oil has increased since those years, as the price has fallen. But it seems likely that Vermonters will keep their knowledge of how to cut, split, stack and properly season firewood, should they need those skills in the future. A 1984 survey by the State of Vermont found that many of the households with no wood-burning facilities were planning to install them, just in case oil prices should rise again.

There is a down side to wood burning: more house fires. State police and Public Service Department figures suggest that woodstove-related structural fires and chimney fires are on the rise, and the Middlebury Cooperative Insurance Co. offers one statistical benchmark. That company attributed 10 percent of its home property losses to woodstove-related fires in 1975. By 1980, the company was attributing 50 percent of such losses to woodstoves and related fires. The problem? Wood fires—especially wood fires using green wood in airtight stoves—create creosote, a gummy flammable material that can collect in chimneys and cause fires. Woodstoves also create more fire hazards such as hot coals, and flying sparks than do other forms of heat.

Wood-generated electricity became a reality in 1985, when the McNeil Plant, a wood-fired power plant in Burlington's Intervale, began generating power. Unfortunately, the plant also caused complaints from its neighbors because of the stench generated when its pile of wood-chip fuel began to ferment. Officials worked to fix the problem and predicted the plant would ultimately win acceptance.

Are Vermont's forests capable of withstanding the renewed demand for wood without sustaining environmental damage? This question was researched in the 1970s by state forestry officials and, to the surprise of many, the answer turned out to be yes. In fact, say forestry authorities, with proper practices, firewood harvesting is good for most Vermont forests, since the state's woodlands are immense, expanding and under-utilized.

More than three-fourths of Vermont is now forested. That is a reversal of the situation 150 years ago, when three-quarters of the state was open farm land. With the exception of a few designated wilderness areas, the forests can benefit from a careful program of firewood and timber harvesting, since wood is a renewable resource.

Wood, as this Cabot logger and his steaming horse both know, is the fuel that
heats you twice.

ROBERT FROST: Vermont's Poet

R obert Frost, once thought of as a conventional nature poet of northern New England, especially Vermont, was actually a writer of many moods and considerable complexity. He has remained close to the hearts of Vermonters, however, because he successfully captured so many truths about the life lived here in language that is as clear and graceful as a mountain stream.

Born in California in 1874, Frost came to New England as a boy, did well in public school, but walked away from Dartmouth College after less than a year and, aiming to be a writer, took up farming in rural New Hampshire. He failed at a series of occupations, quietly writing poems all the while, and in 1911 made a do-or-die decision to live in England for a year and write. His first book of poems, *A Boy's Will*, was published there, and in no time Frost's literary career began. He subsequently became one of the most popular and beloved writers America has ever known. His place in the American literary world seems to be established.

Frost was popular not only for his poetic skills and the depth of his thought, both of which are considerable. His poetry also epitomized a rural America that was dying out—and that therefore was held all the more valuable. Such poems as "Mending Wall," "Stopping By Woods," and "Birches," summed up rural experience for a country that very much wanted to hold onto its rural traditions.

The irony is that many of his finest poems also speak to the dark side of country living—the hard lives, desperate futures and fierce poverty faced by many of the people living in his chosen spot, "North of Boston." Even so, Frost himself had a puckish, elliptical side that made him deny or gloss over the darker side of works like "Out, Out . . . ," and "Home Burial."

His poetry is remarkable for its pungency, its hidden complexities, and the huge range of human feeling and experience it depicts under the cover of its surface rurality. It has become part of the American literary heritage, even as it remains emblematic of Vermont.

Places such as this tumbled Cavendish wall bring Robert Frost to mind for many.

In fact, he defined the Vermont experience so precisely that his poems remain valid and immediate 50 years after they were composed. Vermonters can hear themselves and their neighbors in his longer poems, and can catch glimpses of their state in phrases scattered through dozens of poems.

The restricted view in a forest he sees as "all in lines/ straight up and down of small slim trees/ Too much alike to mark or name a place by."

The cottages he passes on a winter's walk are "up to their shining eyes in snow", and the tiny brook in June has "run out of song and speed."

He wrote of the "dark days of autumn rain" that are "beautiful as days can be," the first snowstorm of the year when he saw "snow falling and night falling fast, oh fast," and the mountain that cradles the town "as in a shadow . . ." All are familiar to Vermonters who have seen such sights themselves and find Frost's recollections of them telling and accurate. His "Spring Pools," for example, describes the woodlands of early spring in words as graceful as they are realistic:

Spring Pools

These pools that, though in forests, still reflect
The total sky almost without defect,
And like the flowers beside them, chill and shiver,
Will like the flowers beside them soon be gone,
And yet not out by any brook or river,
But up by roots to bring dark foliage on.

The trees that have it in their pent-up buds
To darken nature and be summer woods—
Let them think twice before they use their powers
To blot out and drink up and sweep away
These flowery waters and these watery flowers
From snow that melted only yesterday.

CALVIN COOLIDGE
IN THE VERMONT TRADITION

T wo Vermonters have become President of the United States, Calvin Coolidge and Chester A. Arthur. Both were born in Vermont, both achieved prominence elsewhere, and both eventually occupied the White House after serving as vice-president. And there the similarities end.

Coolidge and Arthur were as different as two people could be. Arthur, though raised on a remote farm in Fairfield, became a hefty, city-loving bon-vivant whose presidency is hardly remembered today. By contrast, Coolidge stayed in touch with his farming heritage until the end of his days. Even after he was president, he returned often to his native Plymouth, donned a farmer's smock, and helped with haying or plowing. He was canny enough to make sure there was a photographer around to record such moments.

Coolidge was a popular president and though he went into political eclipse after he left the White House, the approval of a more recent conservative Republican, Ronald Reagan, has rekindled interest in the president from Plymouth.

He was the only president born on the Fourth of July. That was in 1872, in the village of Plymouth Notch. In elementary school, although he was in the upper half of his class, he wasn't outstanding. "He wasn't particularly brilliant or otherwise in school," said one classmate in later years. "He was neither popular nor unpopular. He wasn't a leader in anything."

President Coolidge liked animals. In the White House he had a cat named Tige, which he sometimes carried draped around his shoulders. Coolidge also kept dogs in the White House, and another pet, Rebecca the Raccoon, dined on shrimp and chicken from Mrs. Coolidge's bathroom floor. Grace Coolidge, who hailed from Burlington, was a bright young woman whom Coolidge met in Northhampton, Mass.

Coolidge had a trenchant, understated sense of humor that went right by most of the country. Known for his quips, young Calvin was regularly asked to play end-man in school minstrel shows because of his clowning ability. Was Coolidge abrupt and shy in his relations with others? Perhaps. But he could also be terribly funny, even after becoming president.

Once, as president, he was presented with a handmade rake as a gesture honoring his farming background. The bestower went on at length about the qualities—strong and unyielding, like the president—of the hickory from which the rake was made. He handed the "hickory" rake to the president, who looked it over carefully and turned to the audience:

"Ash," Coolidge said, smiling only slightly.

And yet his life was repeatedly touched by tragedy. His mother died when he was still a boy. A close and dear companion died a scant five years later. His son, Calvin, died of blood poisoning after a trifling injury; the boy had blistered his toe while playing lawn tennis on the White House grounds. In commenting upon the death, Coolidge's terse words and stern faith still tear at the heart:

> In his suffering he was asking me to make him well. I could not. When he went, the power and the glory of the presidency went with him.
>
> The ways of Providence are often beyond our understanding. It seemed to me that the world had need of the work that it was probable that he could do.
>
> I do not know why such a price was exacted for occupying the White House.

After the stock market crash of 1929 plunged the country into a depression and changed American financial life forever, the Republican administrations which had preceded it were criticized. Coolidge, according to his biographers Frank Lieberman and Will and Jane Curtis of Woodstock, seemed tired and depressed. "I do not fit with these times," he said.

Nevertheless, he is remembered with affection, both in Plymouth and elsewhere. Coolidge has been called Silent Cal, and perhaps he was. Yet he has more lines in *Bartlett's Familiar Quotations* than many another president. His economy of words and his wit have lasted.

Phaneuf/Gurdziel

A president's beginnings: Calvin Coolidge's place of birth, just beyond the church, in the tiny village of Plymouth Notch.

FALL FOLIAGE

Vermont's most spectacular display of natural beauty is also its most transient. The brilliant colors of fall foliage last only a few weeks, beginning when late summer becomes early autumn.

However, the foliage connoisseur knows that there is not one foliage season, but three, perhaps four, each with its own beauty. They follow one another from late September until mid-November. First, there is the early show of a few bright preliminary trees, displaying their colors against the brassy-green, late-summer hillsides. More and more trees change as the days shorten and the weeks march on until the precise moment (usually in early October) when it seems that the color has reached its richest. Peak color, partly a subjective notion, marches from north to south through the mountains and is reported on in detail by local newspapers and television stations as it passes. Not long after that, a steady October rain, a day of high wind, or both, are sure to fade the vivid reds and oranges to pastel. The softer, subtler colors sometimes last into November, turning to pale yellows and browns before the leaves finally fall, leaving the hillsides to November's muted shades of gray and purple. Each stage of the changing foliage has its own beauties, and each has inspired poets and painters to create beauty of their own.

But why do the leaves change color? And why are they especially beautiful in Vermont? Jack Frost, hailed in popular song and legend as the painter of the leaves, actually has little to do with the process. Frost and bright foliage occur at the same time largely by coincidence. It is the shortening days of fall and the changing patterns of weather that actually bring on the changing colors.

As daylight gets briefer, deciduous trees begin withdrawing nutrients from their leaves into their trunks and branches to store them for the coming winter. The leaves' green chlorophyll breaks down and yellow xanthophylls (pigments that have been in the leaves all along) are unmasked. The leaves of some trees, such as birches, simply turn yellow as the xanthophylls are revealed. Others—such as the sugar maple—respond to the cool nights and clear days of fall by producing another pigment, anthocyanin, which is red. It helps produce the bright oranges, reds, and purples that highlight Vermont's annual autumnal display.

Bob Davis

Autumn's colors, seen here at Willoughby Lake in Westmore, last but a few
weeks at best. Vermont's most spectacular natural phenomenon—the
changing of the leaves—is its most brief.

Vermont's fall foliage is among the most spectacular in the world, primarily because of the large number of sugar maples, about 34 percent of the forest. Maple foliage, which in fall ranges from flaming orange to bright scarlet, depending upon the heredity of the individual tree, is the brilliant base for the more subtle yellows of beech and aspen, the oak browns, and the purples of ash.

Vermont's open farm fields and cultivated valleys offer good views of every maple-brightened hillside, a configuration of landscape that helps show the fall colors off to best advantage. And since Vermont's mountains are smaller than those to the east or west, more of their flanks are covered with deciduous forests—instead of the great higher-altitude stands of dark, unchanging evergreens.

When is the best time to see the foliage? It depends. There are delights in every stage of the progression of color. But former Gov. Deane C. Davis, a man who knows as much about Vermont as anyone, used to say that October 4 was the day, no matter what the year. If you came to Vermont on October 4, Davis said, you'd see plenty of colorful foliage.

TRAVELERS IN THE GREEN MOUNTAINS

V ermont has long been, as poet Hayden Carruth has noted, a land of passage. For more than 300 years, people have traveled through the state, come to visit, explore, or come to stay. Beginning with the first Europeans, several successive waves of settlers and visitors have traveled through here. From even the earliest of their writings, a recognizable Vermont emerges, different, but not totally dissimilar from the one known today.

There was the Frenchman, Samuel de Champlain, who in 1609 explored the long lake glimpsed earlier by Jacques Cartier from atop Mount Royal, on the site of present-day Montreal. Although he was drawn into a war then being waged between Abenaki and Iroquois, Champlain was clearly charmed by the large and beautiful body of water surrounded by mountains. He described it in glowing terms and, with little modesty but unerring judgment, gave his discovery his own name.

More than 150 years later, Ira Allen saw the economic and strategic potential of the pine-covered terraces above Burlington Bay. "Burlington would, from its situation, become a place of consequence," he wrote, and speculated in hundred-acre lots on the site.

In 1784, Elias Smith, a boy whose family had struggled through the wilderness to Woodstock, wrote about having to subsist on flour and milk, and working all day in the fields into the bargain. If they had only had a few potatoes, he thought, life would have been comparatively rich. With wry humor leavened by experience, he later wrote of his arrival in the new land:

> We, to our great joy, arrived at the town we set out for, which was represented to me as resembling the Land of Canaan; a land of hills and valleys, flowing with milk and honey. The first part I found true.

The Rev. Nathan Perkins found his pleasant home in Hartford, Conn., "a paradise compared to Vermont," and promised to become more contented. Even so, he wondered at the settlers' simple happiness:

> When I go from hut to hut in ye wilderness, the people with nothing to eat—to drink—or wear—all work, & yet the women quiet, serene—peaceable—contented, loving their husbands—their home—wanting never to return—nor any dressy clothes—I think how strange!

That was in 1789. Two years later, John Lincklaen, an early businessman interested in maple sugar, visited then-Gov. Thomas Chittenden and sampled his informal country hospitality.

"He is a man of about 60, destitute of all education, but possessing good sense and sound judgment," Lincklaen wrote. "His house and way of living have nothing to distinguish them from any private individual, but he offers heartily a glass of grog, potatoes and bacon to anyone who wishes to come and see him."

Since the 1800s, famous writers have visited Vermont, making sharp and accurate observations. Nathaniel Hawthorne, in 1835, saw in Burlington a close mix of people that contemporary visitors to the Church Street Mall there might recognize:

> There was a pleasant mixture of people in the square of Burlington, such as cannot be seen elsewhere at one view: merchants from Montreal, British officers from the frontier garrisons, French Canadians, wandering Irish, Scotchmen of a better class, gentlemen of the south on a pleasure-tour, country squires on business; and a great throng of Green Mountain boys, with their horse-wagons and ox-teams, true Yankees in aspect, and looking more superlatively so, by contrast with such a variety of foreigners . . .

Francis Parkman, traveling through Cambridge in 1842, had supper with an old farmer who asked if Parkman were an Indian and questioned him closely about his business, inviting Parkman to stay in his home. Henry David Thoreau in the fall of 1850 rode a train through the state, was disappointed in the small size of the Connecticut River at Bellows Falls, made the unremarkable observation that in the fall the Green Mountains became red, and noted that there was "interesting mountain scenery" in the Ludlow-Mount Holly area "not rugged and stupendous, but such as you could easily ramble over—long narrow mountain vales through which to see the horizon."

Outsiders continued to come to Vermont, after 1900 in sharply increasing numbers. Many came to visit, were charmed by what they found, and moved in. And inevitably, Vermont began to change. "Vermonters are learning that scenery has economic value," said the state Board of Agriculture in 1895. By 1964, the changes had become obvious enough to worry one transplanted Vermonter, writer Noel Perrin. He wrote:

> The life [in Vermont] is so appealing, in fact, that people will pay good money to see it being lived, which is where the trouble begins—there's a conflict of interest here.

But all is not lost yet. Vermont's traditions of equality and laissez-faire community life seem to be surviving. Alistair Cooke notes that all the wealthy people in one southern Vermont town seem to be "summer folks."

"But the summer folks are strangers and underlings," he declares. "The valley has heard many delicate sounds through the years, but it has never heard the advice of a squire or the accent of *noblesse oblige*. The farmers are ruled and rulers. The wealthy stranger goes cap in hand and pays his rates according to Minnie Hoyt and does what Mr. Hoyt says to keep his part of the highway safe and sound . . ."

The collector and editor of the book from which most of these quotations were extracted, Thomas Bassett of Burlington (the book is a delight called *Outsiders Inside Vermont*) offers in that volume a summary of the phenomenon:

> In the long run, it doesn't really matter whether you start from inside or outside a place. In this world there are transients, there are people who just moved in, and there are the rest of us wayfaring strangers.

Inside or outside, that sounds like Vermont.

THE QUESTION OF DEVELOPMENT

In some ways, the contemporary era in Vermont can be said to have begun in 1969, when then-Gov. Deane C. Davis was conducted on a drive through southern Vermont. On that tour, he saw some shoddy second-home developments that shocked him and made him worry about the future of his native state.

Davis's concern, publicity about the new developments, and a concerned state legislature combined in 1970 to create the landmark development-control law still known as Act 250. Despite the publicity surrounding the law, it takes a moderate course in controlling development; it does not ban it outright, but requires compliance with basic environmental standards governing water quality, land use, traffic volume and aesthetic impact.

Vermont is different from many rural places because it is bounded on three sides by major urban centers and is within a day's drive of more than 20 million people. In one sense, the state is a green belt for Boston, New York, Montreal and the other cities surrounding it. Its smallness and pastoral beauty are deeply appealing to city dwellers looking for skiing adventure or a quiet summer vacation. This once-isolated state now finds itself the focus of a major recreation industry that has brought a new level of economic prosperity—even as it has thrown into question many of the state's long-held values and assumptions.

Planner Richard Cowart of Calais reported in his study of the problem that vacation-home and suburban development in Vermont were getting out of control. He said:

> Today, in 1985, the State of Vermont is beginning its third consecutive decade of sustained, rapid development. It is now time to realize that after 100 years of slow change, we are transforming the economy and landscape of our state—in the space of a single generation. Yet Vermont lacks a cohesive growth policy to guide this unprecedented development, or to control the undesirable effects of this largely beneficial growth.

Nevertheless, Vermont remains, in the words of social observer and newspaper columnist Neal Peirce, "The Beloved State," a place capable of inspiring loyalty and

Ann Day Heinzerling

Two economies confront one another across the Mad River Valley. Farms and ski trails: are they mutually exclusive?

affection from both native Vermonters and newcomers alike. Its pastoral beauty, strong sense of community, and social ethic of personal independence and tolerance for individual difference have proven powerfully appealing, and have doubtless helped in establishing the state's strong body of environmental law.

Vermont faces unprecedented development pressures. But there are signs that Vermonters are again responding to protect it. As recently as 1986 the legislature strengthened several state environmental statutes, and concern about development was increasing.

THE REAL VERMONTERS

W hat is real Vermont? Who are the real Vermonters? Such questions crop up frequently these days because of the rapidity with which Vermont is changing. *Real Vermonters Don't Milk Goats* by Frank Bryan and Bill Mares, with its witty one-liners ("Real Vermonters don't flinch when they snap on the jumper cables"), is the most popular book of Vermont humor in recent years, a fact that testifies to both the appeal of the book, and the fascination of Vermonters nowadays with the question of who is and who isn't bona fide.

Unfortunately for anyone interested in firm definitions, this is a subjective question and always has been. In fact, "real" Vermonters are those who are willing to live here year-round, live in an upright, face-to-face way, and make a commitment to their community.

By those commonly accepted standards, pianist Rudolph Serkin, who lives in Marlboro, performs in the music festival that has made Marlboro world famous, and regularly gives benefit concerts for local causes, is as much a real Vermonter as former Gov. Deane C. Davis, who tops nearly everyone's list as the embodiment of Vermont character and values.

However (an important "however"), Davis has ties to something that Serkin has very little connection with, if any: Old Vermont, a complex, wonderful, nearly indefinable heritage. Old Vermont—Vermont's rural folk culture—was largely formed in the nineteenth century, lasted in places well into the twentieth, and today is very rare and therefore of great value. It was a product of a different time, different values, a small-scale economy, and machines that ran on gears, not diodes. Its horsepower wore horseshoes.

Since this heritage contributed so much to the world of rural Vermont idealized today, there is a strong temptation to sentimentalize it and see it through a haze of trivializing nostalgia. That is a mistake, since Old Vermont had its dignity, its darkness, and its worth; it centered not around sentiment, but around work, the real fundamentalism of the time.

Long, long books could be written about any aspect of Old Vermont. These are a few (admittedly subjective) memories of that world:

- Prize speaking: memorizing a poem or soliloquy or heroic passage from literature and reciting it in the grade-school assembly hall for parents and teachers. The best reciter won a prize.

- Kitchen tunks and barn dances: homemade fun when an uncle who could play the fiddle and a cousin who could play guitar got together with someone who played the spoons, and several other people from the farms nearby joined in to make music and dance.

- The day the teacher, Emma Lilley, chased Will Emery out of school with a broom for talking back, and told him never to come back there again. And he didn't.

- Chicken pie suppers at the Grange; or band concerts on the town green, when knowing all the people in the band was easy because they were relatives and neighbors. Youngsters ran around and around the bandstand until they were dizzy, and older people sat in their cars around the green and beeped their horns at the end of each tune.

- Walking to school, usually more than a mile. (Nearly every adult who grew up in Vermont before 1960 has stories about this. It was a character-builder in the pre-bus days. It was not particularly noble; it was just cold as hell.)

- Haying, hayrides, jumping in the hayloft. The horse was slow and meditative pulling the wagon back to the barn. He clopped carefully along, well-acquainted with every turn of the dirt road, every clump of grass.

- The milk-glass hen in the parlor, the big green salt-cellar with the tin top (it must have held a quarter-pound of salt), the treadle sewing machine in the living room, the pantry with doughnuts in the bean crock.

- And the songs, the stories, the music, the joking, the fun.

Robert J. Alzner

Harrowing proceeds, with some fits and starts for repairs, adjustments, and discussion, on a windy Reading hillside.

Vermont was rural and behind the times then. It was brought into the twentieth century by television (which gradually ended homemade forms of entertainment like kitchen tunks and prize speaking) and high-speed interstate highways (which made Vermont accessible to the outside world and vice versa). Such modern conveniences have homogenized much of America's regional strength, and Old Vermont is all but gone. Yet some links to that older world can still be found:

- The closeness to nature Vermont living seems to demand. Even though most Vermonters no longer farm, they take walks, ski, picnic, hike, hunt and fish. It is impossible to get completely away from nature after all, and Vermonters still must deal with the demands of a harsh climate. Nearly half split wood and feed woodstoves, and many still keep a well-trimmed kerosene lamp in a handy cupboard in case the power goes out.

- Contra dances: Both the older Vermonters who perform the intricate dances at fairs and other gatherings as a demonstration and the new crop of contra dancers who dance in grange halls and town halls (and sometimes even barns) for fun. Are they enthusiastic? Ask the people who attend dawn dances—all night contra dance parties—each spring in Calais and Brattleboro.

- The Vermont legislature: The realest of real Vermont. Vermont's citizen legislators are as good a cross-section of the state as can be found. Among favorites over the last 10 years were Ernest R. "Stub" Earle, a conservative Republican from Eden who chewed tobacco, drove Christmas trees to New York in cowboy garb, and ran a snack bar on Lake Eden in the summer; Brian Burns, a Burlington Democrat who lost a primary campaign for governor, but on a good day could play the House of Representatives like a musical instrument; and "Red" Hooper of Johnson, a fabled hunter turned game-warden who did not usually say more than two words in a row, but when he did, was always listened to because he spoke with pungency and wisdom.

- Graham Newell of St. Johnsbury, a history professor and Latin teacher at Lyndon State College and St. Johnsbury Academy. Newell was born and raised in Caledonia

County and though he has traveled widely, still lives in his home town because he prefers to. A quiet, erudite, and civilized man, he knows volumes about Vermont, and notes: "If you have to ask what a Vermonter is, you'll never know."

- Glendon, Gordon and Marjorie Pierce, storekeepers, of North Shrewsbury. Now elderly, they have run Pierce's Store in that little village all their lives. Their quiet decency, their wonderful font of memories, and their love for their town and its history continue to be an inspiration to those lucky enough to know them.

- Town meetings: Well, some town meetings. Held in early spring, Town Meeting is the time local people get their say about local governance. While some town meetings have deteriorated into little more than voting and going home, others still last all day, feature a community dinner at noontime, and are sometimes entertainment as good as a feature movie.

- Country fairs: Especially the smaller ones that are still thoroughly rural. Animals, arcades, outrageous junk food, and a variety of people that seems to congregate only on the midway. The Vermont State Fair at Rutland is big and comprehensive. Barton and Tunbridge Fairs can be a bit seamy. The Caledonia County Fair is often a delight, has lots of character and a cavalcade of farm animals led by local youngsters.

- Going to deer camp. The best ones keep drinking to a minimum, have a lot of talk and a lot of card-playing, and help pass woodland skills from older to younger family members.

- Country stores: A barometer of changing Vermont, in Sherburne they sell T-shirts and tiny tins of maple syrup; in Greensboro, groceries and jumper cables. Either way, they will tell you where you are.

- And (still) the songs, the stories, the music, the joking, the fun.

TOURING VERMONT

F or native or newcomer, the pleasures of driving through Vermont are many and varied. The tours described on the following pages are designed to give both beginners and those familiar with Vermont a sense of its tremendous variety. Each drive, whether long or short, will introduce the traveler to some pastoral views, some pleasant villages, and a taste or two of Vermont history

The tours cover most of the state's geographic regions. But it is not necessary to do them all to get a feel for Vermont. A single tour—or even part of a tour—taken thoughtfully, with time allowed for lunch and rest stops, is bound to be much more rewarding than any attempt simply to rack up as much mileage as possible. A leisurely pace has a side benefit also: it will allow time to meet Vermonters, as well as Vermont. For many travelers, that's the best part of the journey.

Valley Views and Mountain Views
Franklin and Lamoille Counties (approximately 50 miles)

Starting in St. Albans, drive south on Route 104 through open farmland to Fairfax, heart of a major dairying and maple sugaring area. Continue east on 104 to Cambridge and Jeffersonville in the shadow of Mount Mansfield, Vermont's highest mountain. Side roads in this area are often spectacularly scenic.

Then turn left onto Route 108, and proceed about four miles beyond through Bakersfield to the marked left-hand turn to Bordoville and the birthplace of President Chester A. Arthur. Continue westward to Fairfield on this unnumbered road.

At Fairfield, pick up Route 36 and follow it west to St. Albans. Don't miss the sudden, sweeping view of St. Albans, Lake Champlain and the Adirondacks at the brow of a hill just a few miles west of Fairfield. Stop, catch your breath, and drive down the hill to your starting point.

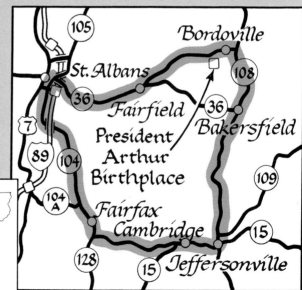

Quiet Lakes and Small Villages
Caledonia, Orleans and Lamoille Counties (approximately 115 miles)

From Hardwick, go north eight miles on Route 14 and take the right-hand turn just north of Lake Elligo to Craftsbury and Craftsbury Common. Stop at the scenic hilltop common and walk around. This is an especially beautiful small village. Then follow the main road north, back to Route 14 and drive north through open Orleans County farm land and the villages of Albany, Irasburg and Coventry.

At Coventry, pick up Route 5 and follow it north to the small but bustling city of Newport on Lake Memphremagog. After exploring (and possibly having lunch) there, leave by driving west on Route 105 to North Troy.

At North Troy, turn right and continue on Route 105A for a short loop into Quebec. You will re-enter the United States at East Richford. Go east on Route 105, over the northernmost shoulder of Jay peak, and to Troy via Routes 105 and 101.

From Troy take Route 100 south through Lowell and Eden to its junction with Route 15 at Hyde Park. The village itself is just off Route 15 and is worth a visit for its attractive Lamoille County Court House and other architecture.

Three miles to the east is Morrisville, where there is an excellent historical museum in the Noyes House. Or return directly to Hardwick along Route 15, which follows the Lamoille River Valley.

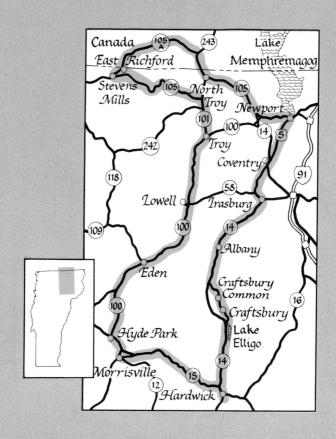

Rural Northeast Kingdom, a Place Apart
Orleans, Essex and Caledonia Counties (approximately 150 miles)

This is a day-long tour of the state's remote northeast corner. Start in St. Johnsbury, but before you begin driving, walk around this small, elegant city. The Fairbanks Musuem and the Athenaeum are among the many delights of the city's upper level. Begin your drive east on U.S. Route 2 through Lunenburg and north on Vermont Route 102 to Guildhall's charming common, which is a good spot for a stop to stretch your legs.

For the next 37 miles, Route 102 winds its way north through countryside that is among the most rural in Vermont. The two small twin villages of Canaan and Beecher's Falls mark Vermont's most northeastern corner. At Canaan, take Route 114 past Wallace Pond and Great Averill Pond to tiny Norton, then continue 13 miles south to the junction of Route 111.

Turn right onto 111 and drive through Morgan Center at the north end of Seymour Lake. Continue westward to Derby Center. At this point, you're just five miles east of Newport, Vermont's northernmost city and an interesting side trip.

From Derby Center, take Route 5A through West Charleston and around the east side of Lake Willoughby, one of the most scenic lakes in the Northeast. The thriving village of West Burke is but a few miles further south, at the junction of Routes 5 and 5A. Follow Route 5 to Lyndonville, an attractive college town.

Then for a few last views, take Interstate 91 from Lyndonville south to St. Johnsbury, your starting point. *Note:* For a two-day tour of northeastern Vermont, plan to stay overnight in Newport, and do the tour on the preceding page one day and this tour the next, both starting from Newport.

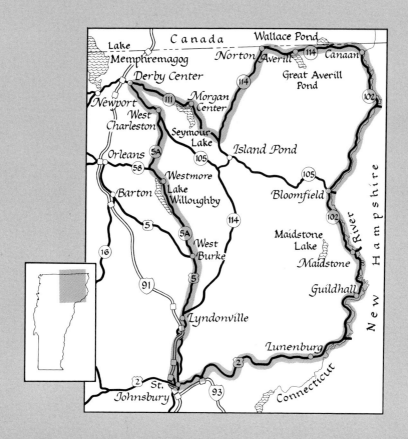

The Champlain Valley's Broad Vistas
Chittenden, Addison and Rutland Counties (approximately 115 miles)

From Interstate 89's Exit 12 in Williston, south of Burlington, drive south on Routes 2A and 116 to Hinesburg. At the south end of Hinesburg, instead of following 116 when it turns sharply left, continue straight ahead on the paved, unnumbered road that leads directly south to the lovely little hilltop village of Monkton Ridge. There are an old meeting house and some fine views of the valley from this picturesque crossroads.

Continue south through East Monkton and about four miles from there take the left to Bristol. From Bristol, drive directly west on Route 17 to U.S. Route 7 and turn south (left). It is eight miles to Middlebury, a beautiful village with many attractions, including Middlebury College. Just four miles out of town is the University of Vermont's Morgan Horse Farm.

After exploring Middlebury, head south on Route 7. In seven miles, turn left onto Vermont Route 53, which swings east, around the far side of Lake Dunmore. There is a nice beach at Branbury State Park. Continue south on Routes 53 and 73 to Brandon, a busy village rich in historic architecture. Continue west on Route 73 through Sudbury and Orwell to Route 22A, a main road through the most rural parts of the Champlain Valley.

Two interesting side trips that branch westward from this road feature important Vermont historical sites. Neither Mount Independence, north of Chipman's Point in Orwell, nor Chimney Point in Addison is highly developed, but both are fascinating lake shore places worthy of a visit. Our prescribed route follows Route 22A north through picturesque Shoreham, Bridport, Addison and Vergennes, where we rejoin U.S. Route 7 for the return trip to Burlington.

For a last view of the valley and lake, drive up Mount Philo in Charlotte, walk the quarter mile to the edge of Philo's cliffs, and take it all in. From Burlington, a tour of beautiful Grand Isle County also makes a rewarding trip.

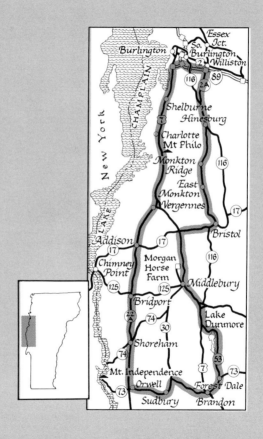

Vermont Heartland: The Central Highlands
Washington, Addison, Windsor and Orange Counties (approximately 120 miles)

From Montpelier, follow U.S. 2 west to Middlesex, then turn south on Route 100B, which merges with Route 100 in eight miles. Sit back and enjoy the pastoral views of the Mad River Valley and beautiful little Waitsfield, which despite much development has retained its charm.

South of Warren, Route 100 plunges through the forested and deep-sided Granville Gulf with its delicate waterfall, Moss Glen Falls. The road emerges into another 15 miles of valley farm land, passes through Rochester, a small village with a pretty common, and meets Route 107 in Stockbridge. Turn left onto Route 107, and follow it to its junction with Route 12 at Bethel.

Take Route 12 north to Randolph, then take a right onto Route 66, and follow it uphill to Randolph Center, a hilltop hamlet where settlement in Randolph began. Go directly north from Randolph Center along the Ridge Road to Brookfield and its unique Floating Bridge. Continue northward on the dirt road that goes through the small village (though it still hews to the ridge, it is known locally as the Northfield Road and Stone Road) and ultimately joins Vermont Route 64 near Exit 5 of Interstate 89.

Turn right, downhill, away from I-89, and proceed to Williamstown and Route 14. Barre's world-famous granite quarries make an interesting side trip. Follow Route 14 into and through Barre, Central Vermont's major industrial center.

Continue through Barre to East Montpelier, then on through North Montpelier. Two miles beyond this small pondside village, there is a left-hand turn onto an unpaved road to Kents Corner and the Kent Museum, open July through Columbus Day weekend. From this classic rural four-corners, continue west one mile to Maple Corner, turn left, and follow the County Road roughly 10 miles back to downtown Montpelier.

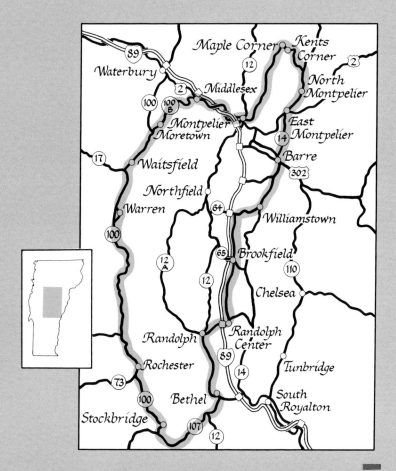

Classic Villages of the Piedmont
Orange and Windsor Counties (approximately 95 miles)

This tour visits several of Vermont's most beautiful villages. It starts in Woodstock, where Federal era houses surround an oval green. Travel north from Woodstock on Route 12, but leave that road after only one mile, turning right at the "Y" intersection to South Pomfret. At South Pomfret, turn right again at the store and drive three miles up to the scenic hilltop hamlet of Pomfret.

Go through Hewett's Corners (a sharp curve in the road with little identification about two miles from Pomfret) and take an immediate left onto the Howe Hill Road. After about five miles, turn left onto the River Road, which follows the White River upstream to South Royalton, home of Vermont Law School.

Cross the river and take Route 110 directly north through the classic valley towns of Tunbridge and Chelsea, then turn right at Chelsea onto Route 113 through Vershire, Thetford and East Thetford. Here, turn right onto Route 5 and go five miles south to Pompanoosuc.

Turn right again at Pompanoosuc and follow Route 132 eleven winding miles to the village of South Strafford. Don't neglect the three-mile spur to the village of Strafford, one of Vermont's most beautiful villages with its extraordinary pristine Meeting House and the Gothic Revival Justin Morrill homestead.

Then continue down Route 132 to Interstate 89 at Sharon. Proceed south on I-89 to Exit 1 and return to Woodstock via U.S. Route 4 and Quechee Gorge.

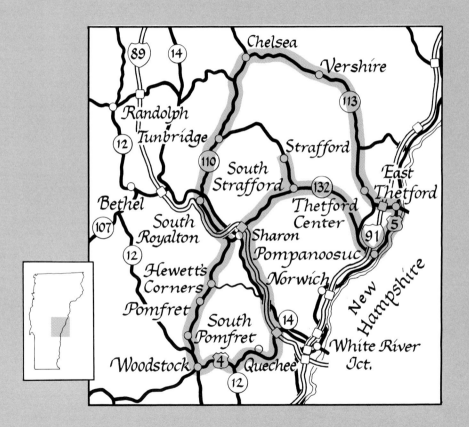

Farm and Forest, Industry and History
Rutland and Windsor Counties (approximately 100 miles)

From Rutland, go west on U.S. Route 4, leaving the limited access highway at Exit 5. Castleton itself is but a mile away. A side trip to the marble quarries in Proctor is also worthwhile.

From Exit 5, proceed north on the unnumbered road to East Hubbardton and the Hubbardton Battlefield, a spot that is both scenic and historic. Continue along that road as it curves downhill and west toward Vermont Route 30 and Lake Bomoseen. Travel south on Route 30, first along the lake, then through farm land, to arrive in the neat college town of Poultney. From there, go east on Route 140 to East Poultney and Middletown Springs, both of which are delightful villages.

Continue on 140 to and through Wallingford, and over the mountains to East Wallingford and its junction with Route 103. Head southeast (right) on 103 past Healdville (where two miles down the side road is an excellent and historic Vermont cheese factory).

Continue to the point where Route 100 branches off sharply to the left and turn onto it. A pleasant 20-mile drive past lakes and mountains follows. The road winds north toward its junction in West Bridgewater with U.S. Route 4. Bear left on Route 4, drive west over Sherburne Pass and down Mendon Mountain to Rutland, where your tour started.

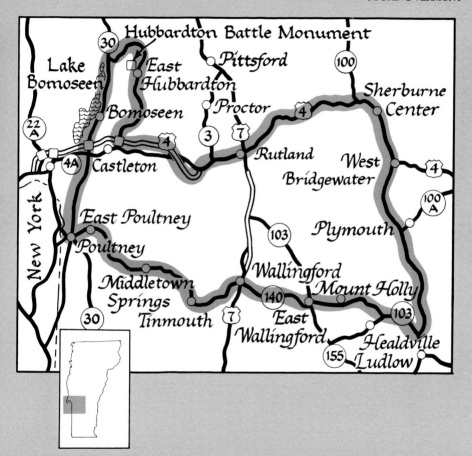

Where Vermont Began
Historic Bennington County (approximately 95 miles)

From Manchester Center, drive south on Historic Route 7A to Manchester Village, a showcase of nineteenth century architecture of which The Equinox resort hotel is the centerpiece. Continue down 7A through Arlington and Shaftsbury, both villages steeped in Vermont history.

At South Shaftsbury, bear right on Route 67 to North Bennington, home of Bennington College. Follow 67A back to Bennington and drive directly downtown, taking a right turn onto Main Street (Route 9). Follow Route 9 west, up the hill and past the Bennington Museum to Old Bennington. Take some time here for the Old First Church and the Bennington Battle Monument.

Then backtrack to U.S. Route 7 north, a limited access road through the mountains that will get you quickly to Manchester Depot. From there, take Route 30 northwest to white-clapboarded, green-shuttered Dorset, a very early Vermont village and still a very beautiful one. Continue north on Route 30 through the Mettowee Valley town of Pawlet.

Two miles north of Pawlet, turn left on the unnumbered road that leads to Route 153. Follow Route 153 to West Pawlet and Rupert, then turn left onto Route 315, which will bring you back to East Rupert and Route 30. Take Route 30 back through Dorset to Manchester Center.

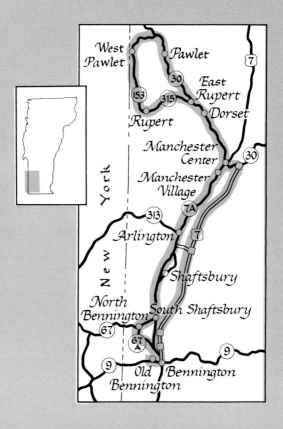

Old Vermont and New Vermont
Windham County (approximately 90 miles)

From Brattleboro, go west and steeply uphill on Route 9, first to Marlboro, a hilltop village where there is a nice small museum of local history a short distance off the main road, and then on to Wilmington, a busy tourist town. In the center of town, turn right onto Route 100 north. Follow this road northward through the heart of southern Vermont ski country.

At East Jamaica, turn right onto Route 30 (south). Go through West Townshend to Townshend and turn left onto Route 35. After about three miles, turn left again, onto the Grafton Road, and follow it to Grafton, a lovingly restored rural village with a beautiful inn at its center.

From Grafton, follow Route 121 southeast along the river valley through the villages of Cambridgeport and Saxtons River. You will come to an intersection with U.S. Route 5 just outside the busy and interesting little city of Bellows Falls. From Bellows Falls, follow either Route 5 or Interstate 91 south to Brattleboro.

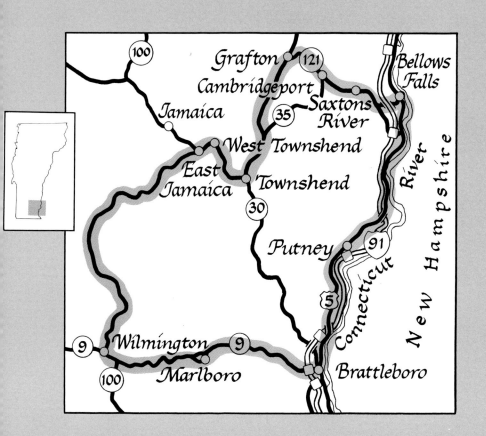

BOOKS FOR FURTHER READING

Bassett, T.D. Seymour. *Outsiders Inside Vermont.* Brattleboro, Stephen Greene Press, 1967. Canaan, NH, Phoenix Publishing.

A collection of excerpts from writings of travelers and explorers in Vermont. Delightful reading, good history.

Biddle, Arthur W. and Paul A. Eschholz, eds. *The Literature of Vermont.* Hanover, NH, University Press of New England, 1973.

An essential book for surveying and enjoying Vermont literature. Although there are some notable omissions, the book remains both useful and pleasurable.

Bruhn, Paul A., compiler. *A Celebration of Vermont's Historic Architecture* (1983) and *A Second Celebration of Vermont's Historic Architecture* (1986). Photography by Sanders Milens. Burlington, VT, Preservation Trust of Vermont.

These two volumes present many of Vermont's most outstanding buildings in superb black and white photographs with incisive text.

Curtis, Jane & Will, and Frank Lieberman. *Return to These Hills: The Vermont Years of Calvin Coolidge.* Woodstock, Curtis-Lieberman Books, 1985.

An entertaining story of Calvin Coolidge's upbringing with a short section on his years as president.

Davis, Deane C. *Justice in the Mountains.* Shelburne, VT, The New England Press, 1980.

A former Vermont governor shares tales from his years before the bar and on the bench in rural Vermont.

Guidebook to the Long Trail and *Day Hiking in Vermont.* Montpelier, VT, Green Mountain Club, 1985.

The most complete information available on hiking in Vermont's mountains.

Hill, Ralph Nading. *Lake Champlain, Key to Liberty.* Woodstock, VT, Countryman Press, 1977.

——, *The Winooski* (Rivers of America Series). New York, Rinehart and Co., 1949.

Hill is Vermont's leading writer of popular history.

——, Murray Hoyt and Walter R. Hard, Jr. *Vermont: A Special World.* Montpelier, VT, Vermont Life, 1968.

Classic photography and several essays about Vermont.

Jellison, Charles A. *Ethan Allen, Frontier Rebel.* Syracuse, NY, Syracuse University Press, 1983.

This biography of Ethan Allen is not only good history, it is good reading as well; witty, entertaining, yet scholarly.

Johnson, Charles. *The Nature of Vermont.* Hanover, NH, University Press of New England, 1980.
Not only a guide to the Vermont environment, an appreciation of it as well.

Lawrence, Gale. *Vermont Life's Guide to Fall Foliage.* Montpelier, VT, Vermont Life, 1984.
Direct, easy to understand explanations of fall foliage by an expert naturalist.

Morrissey, Charles. *Vermont, A History.* New York, W.W. Norton & Co., 1981.
A well-written informal history and appreciation of Vermont.

Perrin, Noel. *First Person Rural* (1978), *Second Person Rural* (1980) and *Third Person Rural* (1983). Boston, David R. Godine, Publisher Inc.
Humorous, perceptive essays about life in Vermont by a Dartmouth English professor and writer who is also a part-time farmer.

Tree, Christina and Peter Jennison. *Vermont: An Explorer's Guide.* Woodstock, VT, Countryman Press, 1985.
Comprehensive guidebook to Vermont.

Vachon, Brian, ed. *Vermont for Every Season.* Montpelier, VT, Vermont Life, 1980.
More color photography and essays about Vermont's seasons and lifestyle.

Vermont Road Atlas, Burlington, VT, Northern Cartographic Inc. 1985.
The definitive road atlas, indispensable for backroad exploration.

ABOUT THE AUTHOR

Tom Slayton is editor of *Vermont Life* Magazine. A seventh-generation Vermonter, he attended schools in Northfield, Vt., and Knoxville, Tenn., and graduated from the University of Vermont in 1963. In the course of a 20-year career with the *Rutland Herald* and Barre-Montpelier *Times Argus*, he covered Vermont politics, the state legislature, and a wide variety of environmental and economic issues. He was a roving reporter, traveling the length and breadth of Vermont for several years. Later, as bureau chief of the Vermont Press Bureau, he covered most aspects of state government. He also wrote free-lance articles for a variety of newspapers and magazines and for six years was the Vermont correspondent for the *Boston Globe*. Prior to assuming the editorship of *Vermont Life*, he was editorial page editor of the *Times Argus*. He was assistant editor of the *Sunday Rutland Herald and Times Argus* for eight years, and has won awards from the Vermont Press Association and the New England Press Association. He lives in Montpelier with his wife, Elizabeth, and son, Ethan.

OTHER BOOKS FROM VERMONT LIFE

VERMONT: A Special World. By Ralph Nading Hill, Murray Hoyt, and Walter R. Hard Jr.

VERMONT FOR EVERY SEASON. Edited by Brian Vachon.

MISCHIEF IN THE MOUNTAINS. Edited by Walter R. Hard Jr., and Janet C. Greene. Illustrated by Jane Clark Brown.

MRS. APPLEYARD'S FAMILY KITCHEN: A Treasury of Vermont Country Recipes. By Louise Andrews Kent and Polly Kent Campion.

LAKE CHAMPLAIN: Key to Liberty. By Ralph Nading Hill.

VERMONT LIFE'S GUIDE TO FALL FOLIAGE. By Gale Lawrence.

Vermont Life Magazine, 61 Elm Street, Montpelier, Vermont 05602

Subscribe to

Vermont Life

MAGAZINE

☐ 1 year—4 issues—$7.50   ☐ 2 years—8 issues—$13.95

Foreign postage: $2.00 per year

☐ Payment enclosed.   Charge my ☐ MasterCard ☐ VISA

_____   _____

Account Number   Expiration Date

For a gift subscription, fill out both boxes; if ordering for yourself, fill in the box at left only.

Your Name		Recipient's Name	
Address		Address	
City		City	
State	Zip	State	Zip

Vermont residents please include 4% sales tax for orders to Vermont addresses.
Please allow 8 weeks for delivery.